MARKETING STRATEGY

A Beginner's Guide to B2B Marketing Success

JASON W. SIMMONS

ISBN: 978-1-54390-935-7 (print)
ISBN: 978-1-54390-936-4 (ebook)

DEDICATION

This book is dedicated to my wife, my best friend, my life partner, and soul mate; Husiela Farani-Simmons. I am grateful for your love, friendship, and support. Thank you for pushing me, motivating me, and most importantly thank you for inspiring me to dream big, always.

ACKNOWLEDGEMENTS

I would like to **acknowledge** current and former colleagues, associates, and mentors who have helped me grow and learn in my career. With specific acknowledgements to:

Allison Duquette

Brett R. Frazier

Klaire Marino

Kristine Reed

Liz Wannemacher

Mike Dietrich

Pete Feinberg

Sean McVey

CONTENTS

INTRODUCTION

B2B marketing is in the midst of a rapid evolution. This is happening for a number of reasons: first, advances in technology, media, and the way people consume and access information about company brands, products, and services is significantly influencing buyer behavior. Second, the proliferation of sophisticated analytics tools allows marketers to make more data-driven decisions that improve marketing efficiencies and effectiveness. Lastly, there is growing internal pressure on the marketing function within organizations to become a more strategic partner in driving revenue, establishing client loyalty, and creating positive brand sentiment. In order to succeed in this environment, it is imperative that marketing teams respond to the external and internal pressures by creating sophisticated, relevant, and competitive marketing strategies that produce winning outcomes for their organizations.

As the marketing function evolves into a more powerful and strategic business function due to these advances, it follows that the senior marketing role will evolve into a more powerful and strategic position. In a 2015 Forbes interview, Bruce Rogers, Chief Insights Officer of Forbes and leader of Forbes' CMO Practice, eloquently stated why he believes CMO's will start to transition into more CEO roles: "If you actually look at the job of today's CMO, these transformational CMOs look and act a lot like CEOs. They create a vision, set goals, build consensus, collaborate across the organization, and lead effective implementation that delivers results. It's almost an impossible job because they have three big roles: 1) owner / driver of brand purpose and the mission of the business, 2) owner of the customer and driver of insights generated from data, and 3) organizational leader focusing firm efforts on relentless customer centricity. When you think about it, what part of the business does the CMO not touch? That's why the best CMO roles are very much a CEO-role in training. We've done research around this and high performing CMOs look like CEOs." (Whitler, 2015)

Many marketing leaders would agree with Rogers' view on the role of CMO's and the growing responsibility owned by the marketing organization, and while an entire book can be dedicated to explaining those views, the focus of this particular book is to provide a formula for building and executing competitive, multi-faceted, and robust marketing strategies that drive revenue. Regardless of the size, market, product, service, or industry—anyone who has B2B marketing responsibilities can pick up this book and use the common sense steps to build their own tangible and actionable marketing strategy. This book is intended to be a guide or a high-level user manual you can use to build your own marketing strategy that is applicable and relevant to your organization.

For now, I recommend that before you begin, first determine if this is the right book for you—and if it is, know what you can expect to get out of it.

Who should read this book?

- Anyone who is new to B2B marketing and wants to learn about building and executing a superior marketing strategy in today's competitive B2B environment.

- Any experienced B2B marketing professional seeking a crash-course or refresher on strategic marketing practices.

- Senior leaders who work at SMB's (small and medium-sized businesses) and who have neither the resources nor the people in place to execute on a sophisticated marketing strategy.

- Any business professional who is interested in learning about B2B Marketing.

What is covered in this book?

This book is comprised of 10 chapters that each offer actionable and practical steps you can use to build and execute a thoughtful, effective, and revenue-focused marketing strategy. Each chapter builds on the next, and the book is divided into three sections each with a specific area of focus. Section 1 is Learning-Focused; Section 2 is Building-Focused; and Section 3 is Execution-Focused.

1. Learning about the Market
2. Understanding Stakeholder Priorities
3. Defining Lead & Revenue Goals

SECTION 1: LEARN

4. Building the Buyer Persona Profile
5. Crafting the Message
6. Creating the Content
7. Balancing the Media Mix

SECTION 2: BUILD

8. Implementing the Media Mix
9. Enabling Sales
10. Measuring Marketing Performance

SECTION 3: EXECUTE

How should you use this book?

Each chapter has a *Call-to-Action* section that contains step-by-step instructions you can use to create your own marketing strategy by applying the lessons you learned in that chapter. (If you wish to learn about best-in-class marketing strategies but don't desire to build your own, then feel free to bypass the *Call-to-Action* sections in each chapter).

IDENTIFY YOUR MARKETING GOALS AND OBJECTIVES

The marketing strategy you create will need to align with your current marketing goals and objectives; however, if you don't already know your marketing goals and objectives (for example, you are a brand new employee at a company and just getting started), that's okay. Your goals and objectives will become clearer as you work through the book and begin to apply what you learn to your own unique situation.

For clarity's sake, here is a quick definition of a goal and an objective:

- **Goal:** A *goal* is the desired outcome you set out to achieve.

- **Objective:** An *objective* is the desired action needed to achieve that desired outcome.

For additional context on the delineation between marketing goals and marketing objectives, and how they relate to one another, here are a few examples:

1. *Marketing goal:* To source 20% of sales pipeline revenue through marketing activity

2. *Marketing objective:* To generate a specific number of marketing qualified leads for the sales team to achieve that pipeline revenue goal.

1. *Marketing goal:* To increase media share-of-voice by 10% percent (share-of-voice is the percentage of all web content mentions your brand / company receives relative to your competitors).

2. *Marketing objective:* To generate a specific number of news coverage pieces via press releases, op-eds, and guest blogs to achieve that share-of-voice goal.

1. **Marketing goal:** To improve net promoter score by 5% (net promoter score is the measure of how loyal your existing clients are to your brand).

2. **Marketing objective:** To focus on certain marketing activities that foster and improve client loyalty.

Most B2B marketing strategies have 1 or 2 goals. The primary goal for any marketing strategy should be revenue-centric, such *as sourcing $X amount of dollars in pipeline revenue* through marketing activity; while a secondary goal can be non-revenue-centric, such as *improving brand favorability* in the market. As you work through this book make certain your own marketing strategy has no more than 1 or 2 goals. Having too many goals embedded in your strategy can result in a strategy that lacks clarity, purpose, and vision.

START WITH A BLANK WORKING DOCUMENT UPON WHICH TO CREATE YOUR STRATEGY

When you begin to work on each chapter's *Call-to-Action*, it's recommended that you use an Excel spreadsheet as your working document. (It's okay if you only have a basic understanding of Excel—you won't be doing anything complicated).

This blank working document will serve as your marketing strategy working document.

Create ten tabs in the spreadsheet that correspond to each of the ten *Calls-to-Action* in each of the ten chapters of the book.

Within your marketing strategy working document, complete each chapter's call-to-action using the step-by-step instructions provided in that chapter.

Located in each chapter are visual aids and images that will help you complete each chapter's call-to-action.

Throughout the book in the call-to-action sections, I will reference this working document as your *Marketing Strategy Working Document*. Once you have read all ten chapters and have completed all ten calls-to-action you will have your very own, completed, marketing strategy! **See Table A.** Notice each tab represents each of the ten call-to-actions in the book for each of the ten chapters.

Table A. Marketing Strategy Working Document

A few items before getting started

- There are many approaches one can take when creating and executing a marketing strategy, and many marketing leaders will have their own ideas and insights based on their own experiences and successes. In my years of working in B2B marketing combined with my academic studies, practical studies, and application of marketing, this is the approach I have found to be most effective—although it is not the only approach.

- Many readers of this book will undoubtedly work in different industries, geographies, functions, and roles; and will market products, services, solutions, or a combination of all of these. For purposes of consolidation and ease, I will refer to products, services, and solutions simply as *solutions* throughout the book.

- It is important to read each chapter and each section in the order that it is laid out, rather than jumping ahead or skipping around. It's recommended that you read through each chapter in sequence to fully comprehend the subject and best practices.

- At the end of each chapter, there is a *Chapter Bonus Material* section that includes related information pertaining to that chapter. Part of that section includes my experiences using or working with specific third-party vendors, resources, and tools that have helped me in my marketing efforts over the years. Mentions of those vendors, resources, and tools should not be misconstrued as endorsements; rather it is merely a reflection of those things which I have found helpful for me as a B2B marketer and practitioner, and which you may find helpful too.

- Upon completing the book you should walk away with the insights and knowledge you need to develop your very own marketing strategy. It goes without saying that you do not need a Ph.D. to build a sophisticated marketing strategy—just the desire to create and execute on effective marketing!

SECTION 1:
LEARN

Section 1 focuses on *Learning,* and includes Chapters 1-3. This section will cover material related to learning about the market environment in which your organization is operating, the goals and priorities of your key stakeholders, and the lead and pipeline revenue goals that you will need to work toward. This is a crucial section because it helps lay the foundation for your overall strategy and will provide a starting point on how to begin *building* a marketing strategy, which is the premise of Section 2.

Chapter 1: Learn about the market dynamics and the competitors within the marketplace.

Chapter 2: Learn the priorities of your stakeholders and the importance of embedding those priorities into your strategy.

Chapter 3: Learn how to define lead and pipeline revenue goals so that your marketing strategy is one that contributes to your organization's bottom line.

CHAPTER 1

LEARNING ABOUT THE MARKET

Chapter Overview:

1. Learn About the Market Landscape
2. Learn About Your Competitors
3. Know How to Apply Your Findings
4. Call-to-Action: Document Your Findings
5. Chapter Bonus Material

Before you can build your marketing strategy, you must first have a strong grasp of the market landscape in which your organization is operating, as well as a strong grasp of your competition. Understanding this context is like turning on a light in a dark room—everything becomes instantly visible.

You will more clearly see how your company fits within the marketplace; market projections, forecasts, and growth rates become clearer. Also, the way your competition approaches the market, and the way they position and sell their solution will become better known.

Studying the market and your competitors as the first step before building a marketing strategy is essential because your knowledge needs to be rooted in knowing where the market is, where it is heading, and how you and other competitors fit in to the market.

In this chapter you will learn how to tap into the right resources and implement the best approaches to help you learn more about the market and your competitors.

▶ 1. Learn About the Market Landscape

Understanding the market landscape will help you to navigate your brand, company, or solution into a more competitive position simply by better knowing where the obstacles lie and where the growth and expansion opportunities exist within the market. For instance, you may learn that some buyers in your market are beginning to look for new or different solutions to help them address their problems, thus you can bring awareness to your senior leadership team and begin to address that in your strategy. Here are a few common and recommended resources you can turn to, in order to broaden your market knowledge. It is important that you reference these resources on a continuous basis, because as the market changes and evolves over time, so too, must your marketing strategy.

RECOMMENDED RESOURCES

- Research & Advisory Firms in Your Market
- Industry Thought-Leaders
- Professional Trade Associations & Organizations
- Trade Publications & Industry News

Research & Advisory Firms in Your Market

To understand what is happening in your marketplace it's recommended you seek data, analyses, and reporting that come from research and advisory firms that operate specifically in your market. The information you glean from these sources is bountiful and is often considered the most credible third-party data you will find. It affords you an unambiguous view of your competitors and their performance, as well as insights about the size of the market; market share distribution among the competition; market growth rate, total addressable market, market projections and profitability; and insights about where the market may be going. It is also information that both your senior leaders and competitors likely revere as Gospel.

As an added benefit, the reporting and data these firms produce can serve you in another capacity. If you think about it, strong marketing content always references credible, third-party data to help prove a point, or to position a particular point-of-view. For example, starting a sales presentation, white paper, or video asset with a statistic from a credible source that reads "82% of Chief Technology Officers believe companies should invest in IT system upgrades over the next 2 years" may make your technology buyers pay closer attention to what you are saying (assuming you sell IT software). So, consider these research and advisory firms a valuable resource for many reasons.

Industry Thought-Leaders

If you need to find out whom in your industry is driving the conversation and creating the narrative around what the future of your industry may look like —look no further than to your industry thought-leaders. These thought-leaders are big-picture thinkers with a long-term view of the market—so you can expect to learn a great deal about where they see the market challenges heading, and, likewise, predictions on what future solutions may look like to address those challenges.

By default, thought-leaders are in the best position to influence the opinions of your buyers, so it's best to keep a close eye on them and listen in on the conversations they are driving in your industry. I highly recommend that you follow these thought-leaders on social media, subscribe to their newsletters, and read articles or blogs they have written. By doing this you will gain a better pulse on the market by staying abreast on the latest ideas and innovations that are beginning to emerge.

Professional Trade Associations & Organizations

It's highly likely that your buyers are members of or are associated with specific *professional trade associations* and organizations. Should you have a desire to study the market, then it's recommended you attend their regional or national conferences and participate in the breakout sessions, workshops, and networking opportunities taking place at these events. There you will get face-to-face interaction with buyers, vendors, and thought-leaders alike—all under one roof. As a secondary benefit, these events have a way of validating or invalidating your current message to the market. For instance, if you have consistently been talking to IT buyers about managing multi-cloud deployments, but you learn that everyone else in the market is starting to talk about the importance of AI (artificial intelligence) in creating IT efficiencies, then you may need to refresh your talk track and begin discussing the issues that appear to be top-of-mind for your buyers right now.

Trade Publications & Industry News

Reading trade publications and news outlets specific to your industry will help you to quickly understand the important things happening in your market and that which is impacting your buyers directly. There are likely a wide variety of industry-specific publications that cater to unique audiences—thus, it is not uncommon to have different topics and issues covered by these different publications. For example, some publications may cater to more senior-level buyers or decision makers, and some may cater to more junior-level buyers or influencers; as a result these publications produce slightly different content. This is important to know because as you begin to implement your strategy you will need to decide which publications would make for the best media-buy opportunities (see Chapter 7).

2. Learn About Your Competitors

A *competitive analysis* is the evaluation of your competitors' strengths and weaknesses relative to yours. The end-goal of conducting a competitive analysis is to better recognize how you stack up against your competition. This section will dive into areas around competitor web presence, messaging, content strategy, and media share-of-voice. You can use your findings from this section as a way to create differentiation and distance between you and your competitors once you are ready to begin *building* your marketing strategy (which is covered in Section 2, Chapters 4-7).

COMPETITIVE ANALYSIS TACTICS

- **Media Share-of-Voice**
- **Competitor Content Audit**
- **Search Engine Presence**

Media Share-of-Voice

Media share-of-voice is the percentage of all web content mentions your brand or company receives relative to your competitors. As a formula, this would read:

Your Brand Mentions / TOTAL Market Brand Mentions (you & competitors) = Share-of-Voice Percentage

If your brand was mentioned 100 times in the media over the past 6 months, and the total number of mentions received among you and all your competitors was 500, that would mean that your media share-of-voice is 20%.

100 Brand Mentions / 500 TOTAL Market Brand Mentions = 20% SOV

Conducting a media share-of-voice analysis is an excellent way for you to gain context about how your brand is perceived in the market, how often it is referenced, and how those two criteria compare with your competitors. It is usually the PR teams within organizations who can calculate this. Your PR team can also look at more specific data to determine the qualitative coverage, not just the quantitative coverage. For instance, if your brand commands a strong share-of-voice percentage, but the coverage is primarily negative, it may be more of a hindrance than a help. There are ways your PR teams can factor in the qualitative aspects of media coverage, such as positive and negative coverage, to add additional context to share-of-voice.

To calculate **social media share-of-voice**, the formula can be applied the exact same way, but instead of reviewing online mentions across the entire web, you review mentions strictly on social media platforms. Again, PR teams or social-media marketing teams can obtain this information.

Competitor Content Audit

Conduct a content audit of your competitors to get an idea as to their content strategy as well as the messaging strategy that underpins that content. The low hanging fruit, of course, is to view and explore their website. You should want to find out how a competitor is positioning their brand/solution/company, what their value proposition is, and what makes their offering unique.

In addition to their web content, look for other salient content pieces such as blogs, white papers, other thought-leadership, client stories, and video testimonials. Take note of how their message is positioned to solve problems for buyers. If you stumble across gated content (content that requires a form submission that captures your contact info), download it so you can start receiving their automated nurture emails—you can also subscribe to their blog and get notified when new blog entries are published. A key take-away from the competitor content audit is that you get a view into the content your prospective-buyers are being exposed to and how those buyers may be interpreting your competitors' messages.

Search Engine Presence

To get a real sneak behind the curtain of your competitors' search engine strategy you can turn to specific SEO & SEM (*search engine optimization & search engine marketing*) tools. These tools will allow you to compare and contrast the strength of your competitors' websites and web presence with your own, and gain a better understanding of their overall SEO & SEM strategy. These tools can provide insights into both yours and your competitors: page and domain *authority* scores, third-party sites that link back to the company website, costs for bidding on specific keywords, and keywords that are driving traffic to company websites and landing pages. (SEO and SEM are covered in more detail in Chapters 7 and 8, including how to improve your strategy in those areas).

▶ 3. Know How to Apply Your Findings

You have just spent some time reading about the various resources with which to learn about your competitors and the market landscape. But how can you take the information and make it actionable? How can you apply it practically?

Example: Trade Association Conference Success

Let's say you have just started working for an organization and are new to the business, or perhaps you have been working at your organization for a while, but are being asked to own the marketing responsibilities for a solution that is new to you. You begin to research and study both the market and your competitors and you come to identify three important findings in your research.

First, you learn of a particular trade association that is highly-regarded by your buyers, and that the association will soon be hosting their annual conference. You are certain your competitors are attending. Second, using your SEM web-based tools you find that your biggest competitor has been putting a lot of resources behind their SEM strategy to drive traffic to their website to promote a compelling eBook they have recently written and published. Third, you come to learn that the same competitor recently made a strategic acquisition of another company several months back and it has created a great deal of attention and buzz which is still lingering.

In order to stunt their momentum you decide to huddle up with internal stakeholders to kick around ideas and brainstorm. The first thought that comes to your mind is this trade association conference that's quickly approaching; you feel it's important to make a big splash at the event. You and your stakeholders look at the marketing budget, and toss around ideas and come up with a plan.

Your team decides to: 1) sponsor the conference, thus getting you some brand recognition at the event; 2) issue a press release just days prior to the conference notifying the market of a big-name client your company has just recently signed, and which is sure to turn heads and; 3) find and secure an industry thought-leader to speak at an exclusive dinner you plan to host for key prospects and attendees during one of the evenings at the conference. All of this is agreed upon, and you pull it off–the event is a success.

You get feedback from your executives who attended and they report having had extraordinary results with attendees, and they claim that many conversations were spurred by the press release of the big client your company just signed. The dinner was extremely well attended because everyone was interested in hearing the thought-leader speak; the dinner was also very engaging which resulted in a very productive networking opportunity for the sales reps. All in all, it worked out really well.

If you reflect back on what you got out of this, at a thirty-thousand foot view, it's fair to say the result of this three-prong approach led to: brand recognition and brand elevation (through the conference sponsorship); media awareness and the positioning of your company as a strategic player within the market (through the well-timed issuance of the press release of an important client); and the generation of warm leads and opportunities in the pipeline for the sales team (sponsorship and dinner event featuring a well-known thought-leader).

In this above example, all of this happened simply because you applied what you learned when studying the market and your competitors, then took action to gain visibility. The hypothetical example included everything you learned about in this chapter – from the research you conducted on trade associations so you could know which one to attend, to better understanding which thought-leaders might create a draw with the attendees, to better grasping your competition so you could swing momentum and attention from their direction to yours.

4. Call-to-Action: Document Your Findings

Save what you learn about the market and your competitors by keeping a record of all the necessary findings.

Exercise: Document Your Findings

Using your Marketing Strategy Working Document, record this information by creating a series of columns and label them as indicated below. Then under each column begin to fill it in more fully, row by row. **See Table 1.**

Table 1. Learn About the Market

	A	B	C	D
1	Competitors	Competitor Value Props	Competitor % of Market Share	Media Share of Voice
2	COMPANY X	Value Prop for X	15%	12%
3	COMPANY Y	Value Prop for Y	20%	30%
4	COMPANY Z	Value Prop for Z	8%	15%
5				
6				
7				
8				
9	Research Firm in your Marke	Industry & Market News Outlets	Industry & Market Thought-Leaders	Prof Trade Associations & Organizations
10	Research Firm X	Outlet X	Thought-leader Name & Social Profile of X	Prof Association & Org X
11	Research Firm Y	Outlet Y	Thought-leader Name & Social Profile of Y	Prof Association & Org Y
12	Research Firm Z	Outlet Z	Thought-leader Name & Social Profile of Z	Prof Association & Org Z
13				
14				

1) **Competitors**
   a. List your major competitors—including their websites

2) **Competitor Value Propositions**
   a. List your competitor value propositions

3) **Competitor Market Share %**
   a. List the percentage of market share for each competitor

4) **Competitor Share-of-Voice: Media**
   a. List the share-of-voice percentage in the media for each competitor

5) **Research Firms (specific to your market)**
   a. List all the research firms that conduct research and analyses about your market

6) **News Outlets (specific to your industry & market)**
   a. List all industry specific and market specific news outlets

7) **Thought-Leaders (specific to your industry & market)**
   a. List all of the most high-profile and well-known thought-leaders in the industry, including their websites or social media handles and accounts

8) **Professional Trade Associations (specific to your industry & market)**
   a. List the most prominent professional trade associations and organizations in your industry and market—including their websites

The purpose of keeping a record of your findings is because it will come in handy once you begin to build out the other parts of your strategy (and as you work through the rest of this book). Consider again the *Trade Association Conference Success* example. The information you are being asked to collect in this call-to-action exercise was applicable in that scenario – information about the competitors, who the thought-leaders are, and which trade associations are of most importance to your buyers all played a part in that example. As you can see, there are a number of ways this information will be valuable to you, so be sure to keep it updated regularly and continue to study your competitors and the market.

5. Chapter Bonus Material

Here are some additional best practices and bonus material specific to this chapter:

Growth Share Matrix

A Growth Share Matrix provides deeper context about where and how all of your organization's products and solutions align with the market by plotting them on a graph using two variables. **See Figure 1.** The x-axis represents market maturity, and the y-axis represents how well known your solution is in the market. The shape sizes represent revenue goals of each solution within your company, and the colors represent buyer personas for those solutions.

This Growth Share Matrix can help you determine how to align your marketing approach with where your solution is currently positioned in the market. For example, if your solution is not well known and in somewhat of a new market (upper left quadrant), perhaps your marketing approach should be to educate prospects about their problem. Here, the goal of your message would be to build awareness and trust about your offering. Or, if your solution is very well known and in a very mature market (lower right quadrant), perhaps your marketing approach should be geared toward pursuing competitive takeaways. Here your message would put a stronger emphasis on client success stories, or superior solution features. These growth share matrices can be developed using external consultants, or developed internally using the collective knowledge of people within your organization.

Figure 1. Growth Share Matrix

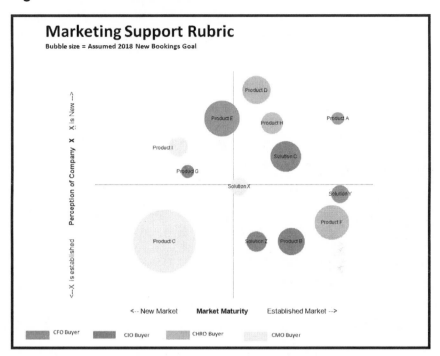

Insider Tips

To help you better learn about the market here are a few resources I have personally found useful for me as a marketer, and that you may find useful too. Look to social media companies such as **Hootsuite** to provide you the tools you need to measure social media share-of-voice, they offer much more than that, but this is one area where they can help with your social media strategy. SEO companies such as **MOZ** offer a plethora of tools to help you up your SEO game; they even offer in-depth SEO training turning you into a better SEO marketer. Lastly**, Trendkite**, a company that specializes in PR analytics, can help you measure your media share-of-voice, and they also provide other services and analytical tools that measure your PR activities and outcomes.

CHAPTER 2

UNDERSTANDING STAKEHOLDER PRIORITIES

Chapter Overview:

1. Understand the Marketing Priorities
2. Identify the Sales Priorities
3. Determine the Product Management Priorities
4. Call-to-Action: Document Your Stakeholder Priorities
5. Chapter Bonus Material

After learning about your competitors and the market, you should spend time learning about the priorities of your key internal stakeholders, primarily the Marketing, Sales, and Product Management teams, with whom you will be working closely. After all, your marketing strategy is about achieving organizational growth and success, so understanding the goals and priorities of your stakeholders, and working toward those collectively, will help you to contribute to that success. It's not to say that you make your stakeholders' priorities your priorities, rather it is about identifying shared priorities and working toward those, together.

In this short chapter you will learn why it's important to ensure your marketing strategy includes the shared priorities of your marketing, sales, and product management stakeholders, and how you may implement shared priorities into your strategy.

▶ 1. Understand the Marketing Priorities

Unless you are working in a company where there is little to no marketing structure, such as a small firm or start-up, then you are likely in an environment where there already exists a functioning marketing organization, and with it some established marketing processes, strategies, and priorities in place. It's critical to know how you may be asked to help contribute to your marketing organization's success.

For instance, there may be an organization-wide push to foster positive brand sentiment with existing clients due to months of negative press coverage. In this case it will be crucial to figure out how you can make improving the company's *net promoter score* (net promoter score is the measure of how loyal your existing clients are to your brand) a priority in your marketing strategy; and to figure out how you can work with Public Relations more closely to promote positive press coverage.

Or, perhaps the organization has recently rolled out a new corporate social responsibility initiative, and now you must find a way to incorporate that message into your own messaging, content, and strategy. These are just a couple of examples of shared marketing priorities you may encounter.

It's recommended that you meet with your marketing leader or other key marketing stakeholder(s), and attempt to understand how they envision success for you and the marketing strategy you are tasked with implementing. You also need to determine what, if any, current organizational marketing priorities need to be embedded into that approach.

Create a regular cadence of meetings with the appropriate marketing stakeholders to discuss updates and topics that have shared relevance, such as updates around new marketing objectives, and the results of marketing campaigns.

▶ 2. Identify the Sales Priorities

There are certainly many shared priorities between marketing and sales, and most of it will be tied to generating or influencing pipeline revenue in some way, shape, or form. When meeting with your sales stakeholder(s) to discuss their priorities, expect for the conversation to quickly turn to how marketing can help source pipeline revenue and create or accelerate more sales opportunities.

Chapter 3 is devoted to defining lead and revenue goals; specifically, how to define a *marketing qualified lead*, how to calculate cost-per-lead, how to estimate conversion of that lead down the pipeline, and how to estimate marketing-sourced pipeline revenue based on marketing budget. This chapter, however, will help you think through the tactical components of marketing campaigns and activities that help the sales team achieve their sales goal, which inextricably will help you reach yours.

For instance, the sales team may be clamoring for a more robust inventory of client success stories to share with their prospects, and thus want to work with you to find those clients and build those success stories. Another example may be a desire to have a larger share-of-voice in the media because the competition is vastly dominating the market in this capacity and are gaining a lot of attention from prospective buyers. Therefore, more work needs to be done build a larger presence in the media via news articles, blogs, and sponsored webinars.

Lastly, there may be a need for the marketing team to host more in-person events, such as small forums where prospective clients, industry leaders, and thought leaders can gather for a day of discussions and content that highlights issues happening in the market. These events would primarily help to accelerate deals that are already in the sales pipeline or to establish new conversations with new prospects (it does this by establishing your company as a thought-leader). As you can see, these are the more tactical components that have the ability to drastically influence sales outcomes. Later, the book will discuss exactly where and how you can embed these into your strategy.

Create a regular cadence of meetings with the appropriate sales stakeholders to discuss updates and topics that have shared relevance, such as new sales objectives, the results of marketing campaigns, updates on how sales reps are managing leads, and feedback on campaign strategy or tactics.

3. Determine the Product Management Priorities

Your product management team will likely have a strong pulse on the market and the competitive landscape; they will of course be experts on your company's products/solutions too. Given that, it's not uncommon for them, like the sales team, to have strong opinions on the marketing strategy and approach. After all, this stakeholder is responsible for building the solution so that it meets the needs of the market—and they want to see it successfully adopted. Because the marketing team is responsible for taking the solution and promoting it in the market, both product management and marketing teams must stay in close communication in order to create a smooth and successful roll out.

When you meet with your product management stakeholder, find out how you can best work together. Learn what goals, priorities, or challenges they have and where you may be able to assist. For example, if a particular feature has not been widely adopted by the market as expected, perhaps the marketing team could put more effort behind the marketing promotion of that feature. Or, perhaps the marketing team could provide the sales team with more effective sales enablement training and collateral that helps them more easily articulate that feature and its value proposition to prospects.

Create a regular cadence of meetings with your product management team to discuss updates and topics that have shared relevance, such as the latest market trends, the results of marketing campaigns, or the results of beta-testing new features or functions.

▶ 4. Call-to-Action: Document Your Stakeholder Priorities

Exercise: Document Your Stakeholder Priorities

Using your Marketing Strategy Working Document create 3 columns. **See Table 2.** Label each column as listed below. Then under each column list 2-3 shared priorities you identified with each stakeholder. Once you get to the other parts of the marketing strategy around building content, developing the *media mix* strategy, and executing that media mix strategy (which is discussed in later chapters) you will need to reference these shared priorities and incorporate them into your plans.

- **Shared Priorities: Sales Team**
- **Shared Priorities: Marketing Team**
- **Shared Priorities: Product Management Team**

Table 2. Understand Stakeholder Priorities

A Shared Priorities: Sales Team (2 - 3)	B Shared Priorities: Marketing Team (2 - 3)	C Shared Priorities: Product Management Team (2 - 3)
Build more case studies / success stories the sales team can reference and use often	Embed new corporate social responsibility message into marketing message	Develop strategy to announce more rapidly to the market new solution features once they are implemented
Host small in-person events / get-togethers targeting key prospects and existing prospects in the pipeline	Foster positive brand sentiment with existing clients	Help build internal training docs with product management team to help train new sales reps
LIST 2 - 3 SHARED PRIORITIES FOR EACH STAKEHOLDER GROUP; ONLY INCLUDE SHARED PRIORITIES THAT YOU HAVE THE ABILITY TO INFLUENCE IN YOUR MARKETING STRATEGY		

 # 5. Chapter Bonus Material

Here are some additional best practices and bonus material specific to this chapter:

Meeting Preparation with Stakeholders

Before meeting with your stakeholders, it might be a good idea to create a list of questions that you would like to ask them. These questions should seek to elicit the type of responses that provide a clear understanding of the priorities they are working toward, and if and how you may play a role in that priority. It's also best to send those questions in advance of the meeting, perhaps several days before, so they can think through it more deeply and engage in more thoughtful dialogue upon meeting with you.

This will go a long way in giving you a very clear view into how your roles may best work together—and ultimately how you can build your marketing strategy in such a way that ensures shared success. Going through this exercise is not only about identifying goals and priorities but also about garnering the much-needed buy-in from these groups for your strategy. The buy-in comes about by virtue of meeting with these groups, soliciting their thoughts, and requesting their input.

This, in essence, creates a sense of collective ownership around the strategy and turns *your* marketing strategy into *our* marketing strategy. This is crucial because when parts of the strategy perform well, everyone shares in the victory, and when parts of the strategy do not perform well everyone shares in the concern and the desire to create a victory.

Meet with Stakeholders after Your Marketing Strategy is Finalized

As you go about creating your strategy, and once you have finalized your plans, it will be necessary for you to share the strategy with these specific groups. This is not only a professional courtesy, but also allows your stakeholders to see where and how you've implemented some of their priorities, which creates more buy-in from these central groups.

CHAPTER 3
DEFINING LEAD & REVENUE GOALS

Chapter Overview:

1. Generating Leads
2. Generating Marketing-Sourced Pipeline Revenue
3. Call-to-Action: Document Your Lead & Pipeline Revenue Goals
4. Chapter Bonus Material

Marketing goals may vary for every B2B marketer. However, all B2B marketers, regardless of their work environment (i.e. organization size, market, industry, geography) will have goals and objectives that are tied to leads and or pipeline revenue. This chapter will help you better understand and calculate your lead and revenue-based goals. These goals can be divided into two sequential components: 1) generating leads; and 2) generating marketing-sourced pipeline revenue (those leads that convert into sales opportunities in the pipeline).

In other words, how many *MQL's (marketing qualified leads)* should you expect to deliver to sales? And, how do those MQL's convert through the sales funnel to *SAL's (sales accepted leads),* and then to *SQL's (sales qualified leads* - which are also known as sales opportunities in the pipeline)?

To answer these questions you first need to know how a lead (MQL) is defined in the organization, what the average cost-per-lead (CPL) is, and how much budget you have allotted for lead-gen initiatives. Once there is clarity around those things you can then calculate how much pipeline revenue you can expect to source by plugging in B2B industry average *sales funnel conversion* rates. It sounds like a lot—and it is—but that's okay because we will take it one step at a time.

In this chapter you will learn everything you need to know about how to define and develop lead and pipeline revenue goals, how to calculate the number of leads you can generate through marketing spend, and how to calculate conversion rates through the sales funnel. The first part of this chapter will show you how to define a lead and determine CPL; the second part of this chapter is about what happens to that lead next.

1. Generating Leads

HOW TO CREATE A LEAD DEFINITION

If you work in a marketing organization where lead definition is ambiguous or unknown, then a good place to start building structure around that definition is with your sales leader. It's imperative that you come to an agreement with sales regarding what exactly constitutes a MQL (marketing qualified lead) for the sales organization. He or she will likely have strong opinions on this subject, so it's best not to define it without their input or agreement.

Because there are many different ways to define a lead, the average CPL (cost-per-lead) can vary drastically, and likewise, the conversion rate of that lead through the sales funnel will vary, too. For context, here are some examples of how a lax lead definition and strict lead definition can impact CPL and conversion rate.

Lax Lead Definition

A lax lead definition can mean a higher volume of leads are produced, which will decrease the overall average cost-per-lead. It also means the rate of conversion through the sales funnel will be *lower* because the lead quality is lower. For instance, if within your organization just about anything will pass as a marketing qualified lead (even if it's someone who may not be that interested or who doesn't have strong buying authority) then you will probably generate a whole lot of leads. This also means that your cost-per-lead is lower, which is great, but the bad news is that because the lead quality is low, then very few of those leads will actually turn into *sales opportunities* in the pipeline. Thus, that conversion rate in the sales funnel is probably pretty low. In fact, it's likely your sales team is rejecting a whole lot of leads because they are of low quality.

A lax lead definition = More Leads = Lower CPL = Converts at lower rates in sales funnel.

Strict Lead Definition

A strict lead definition can mean a lower volume of leads are produced, which will increase the overall *average cost-per-lead*. It also means that the rate of conversion through the sales funnel will be *higher* because the lead quality is higher. For example, if your sales and marketing leaders have very strict guidelines on what actually constitutes a lead; say, they only want a lead who directly expresses interest in your solution, meets very strict qualification criteria, and has been vetted with an inside sales rep. This may mean that you will likely produce just a small handful of leads—it won't be nearly as many as in the previous example. Also, the average cost-per-lead will be much higher because your marketing dollars didn't net that many leads. The good news, however, is that those leads will likely convert at a much higher rate once the sales team gets involved because those leads are of such high caliber.

***A strict lead definition = Fewer Leads = Higher CPL
= Converts at higher rates in sales funnel.***

The best approach between the two is the latter, so put in place a strict lead definition that has more filters rather than fewer filters applied to the qualification criteria. While the sales team will likely receive fewer leads with this approach, the leads they do get will be higher quality. Taking the other approach and providing the sales team with more leads but those that are of lower quality can manifest in lost confidence of the marketing strategy.

A common way to define a B2B lead is through the *BANT* definition. There are many models and acronyms similar to BANT; so it's recommended you use a lead definition that's proven, reputable, and that you're most comfortable with. In this case we'll stick with BANT as it's the most recognized and used most commonly. Here's how BANT is defined:

Budget – Lead has **budget** to purchase

Authority – Lead has buying **authority** or is decision maker

Need – Lead has signaled there is a **need** for a solution

Timeframe – Lead has signaled they are looking to purchase within a particular **timeframe**

A prospective lead that meets the BANT definition is an MQL that is ready for sales. (For this chapter, we will assume all MQL's in our examples meet BANT definition).

Here are some examples of how to screen for and identify BANT through different lead-gen activities:

- Lead attends an industry conference or company-hosted event and through dialogue with sales rep is determined to meet BANT definition.

- Lead participates in content marketing campaign and has engaged with many content assets throughout the *buyer journey* (engaged via email clicks and opens, and more *content downloads*). BANT information was collected through various form fields (job title, company size, and when they are looking to buy) on landing pages and the sales rep who owns that territory follows up on the lead.

- Lead visits your company website on multiple occasions and has then been remarketed. Lead eventually completes a *contact us* form and those fields capture BANT information. The sales reps who owns the territory then follows up with the lead.

- Lead registers for and attends a webinar. An inside sales rep conducts a follow-up call with the attendee to screen for BANT. It is determined they meet the BANT criteria and lead is passed on to the sales rep who owns that territory.

- Lead is actively engaged in a number of random marketing activities such as downloading content, visiting company website, opening emails, registering for webinars etc., but BANT is not fully known. An inside-sales rep follows up on that lead and, through dialogue, the lead is fully vetted for BANT and is passed on to the sales rep who owns that territory.

In the last scenario just provided (in which BANT information may not be fully known, but where there appears to be a considerable amount of marketing engagements taking place), a trigger should be in put place to forward that potential lead to an inside sales rep who can screen it for BANT based on those number of engagements. Again, it's paramount to work with your sales leader to identify how many times a potential lead must engage in marketing activity or content before outreach is conducted. Come to an agreement on how many downloaded pieces of content, hits on a website, or clicks in various nurture emails is sufficient enough to warrant a follow-up call from an inside sales rep. That inside sales rep will then need to further qualify that potential lead for BANT before passing it on to the territory sales rep.

After you've identified with your sales leader how a lead is defined, and when follow-up from the sales reps should occur, start setting up triggers in your *Marketing Automation systems* so that lead scores can be assigned to lead records based on that agreement with sales. Those scores should be comparable to the types of engagements taking place as well as to the quality of the lead as defined by BANT.

For instance, an engagement that included someone attending a webinar should probably be given a higher lead score than an engagement that included someone just opening a marketing email. Likewise, a person looking to purchase (Timeframe) in three months may be of higher value than someone looking to purchase in one year. Lastly, a lower-level job title (Authority) may mean a lower score than a higher-level job title.

The *Marketing Automation system* and *CRM system (Customer Relationship Management system)* administrators can set all this up for you and provide overall guidance and best practices on lead scoring. The types of triggers and engagements you should look for may include: form submissions, event registrations, site traffic hits (cookie-tracking), click-through's, email-opens, and more.

The key takeaway here is to: 1) Define what constitutes a lead–through BANT or some other similar criteria; and; 2) Determine how many number of marketing engagements for unknown BANT leads are needed before passing the lead on to an inside sales rep.

HOW TO CALCULATE AVERAGE COST-PER-LEAD (CPL) POST-CAMPAIGN

$ Budget / # MQL's = CPL

Many organizations calculate the average cost-per-lead by taking the marketing budget that's dedicated to lead-gen initiatives and dividing it by the total number of leads it actually generates. Organizations may include other associated costs as part of that budget, such as costs for developing marketing content, or costs dedicated to hiring inside sales reps to qualify leads. Using this somewhat loose definition, given a $100k budget for a lead-gen campaign that netted 50 MQL's would mean the average cost-per-lead came out to $2k:

$100k budget / 50 MQL's generated = $2k CPL

HOW TO ESTIMATE LEAD VOLUME PRE-CAMPAIGN

$ Budget / $CPL = # MQL Estimation

If you need to estimate or predict the number of MQL's your lead-gen campaign will produce before that campaign begins, simply take the budget you have been allotted and divide that by the average cost-per-lead. This will give you the number of MQL's you can expect to produce. For example, if you have a $100k budget and the average CPL within your company and for your specific solution is $4k (historically), you should expect to deliver 25 MQL's for the sales organization:

$100k budget / $4k CPL = 25 MQL's

HOW TO DEVELOP A COST-PER-LEAD ESTIMATE

What if you don't know your current average CPL, but need to calculate it before you start a lead-gen campaign so you can estimate how many MQL's you can expect to deliver? In that case, it's recommended you turn to outside resources for help. There are many external resources that can help you determine average CPL if you don't already know it. For instance, SiriusDecisions, a consulting firm that specializes in B2B sales, product management, and marketing has developed a highly-respected Lead Spectrum model. This is a complete and thorough model for categorizing leads into different levels of qualification based on lead interest, authority, and propensity to buy. Within each qualification level there is a CPL range that can be utilized.

According to their model, a level 5 lead (the highest qualified lead possible) can range anywhere from $1,700 per lead to $5,500 per lead (B2B industry-average). If you decide to seek outside help to estimate CPL for your organization, be sure to choose a firm that uses the criteria that best aligns with your solution, lead definition, market, and industry.

Over time, and after you've launched some campaigns, you will start to build your own CPL data. That information can then serve as CPL benchmark data for future campaigns and you can begin to eliminate third-party data.

▶ 2. Generating Marketing-Sourced Pipeline Revenue

HOW TO DETERMINE MARKETING-SOURCED & INFLUENCED PIPELINE REVENUE GOALS

Now that you have come to an agreement with your sales leader on the number of leads marketing can expect to deliver to sales, you can begin to further your knowledge of how leads move through the sales funnel and turn into pipeline revenue. This is done by factoring in the sales funnel *conversion rates*. Those rates calculate how a marketing qualified lead converts in the sales funnel beginning with conversion from new lead, then to working lead, to sales opportunity in the pipeline, and lastly to a closed-won deal (though this chapter focuses on pipeline revenue as a goal, and not closed-won revenue as a goal, information will still be provided in this section about how leads may convert through the entire sales journey – from lead to closed-won revenue).

Many B2B organizations expect their marketing departments to *source* about 20% of pipeline revenue and *influence* about 30%. The difference between those two terms is slight:

Marketing-sourced pipeline revenue = a lead generated directly from marketing activity (e.g. lead came from content campaign and was nurtured and passed to sales) and eventually became an opportunity in the pipeline. Marketing sourced that opportunity.

Marketing-influenced pipeline revenue = a lead generated by sales, but marketing played a role after the fact (e.g. lead was acquired by sales through cold-call) but later engaged in some sort of marketing activity such as attended webinar, downloaded marketing content, etc.

If you don't already know what your goal is with respect to the percentage of pipeline revenue you must source or influence, then this would be a good time to work with your marketing and sales stakeholders to determine the goal.

HOW TO DETERMINE SALES FUNNEL CONVERSION RATES

This is an area where your organization may already have some existing data and metrics around conversion rates specific to your organization and solution. Use this data to begin to calculate and predict how many of the leads you produce will make their way through the sales journey ending up as a sales opportunity record with a revenue figure assigned to it.

If information around sales funnel conversion rates does not exist in your organization, then it's recommended you turn to reputable external marketing firms that have data on those rates. Again, you can use an external expert such as SiriusDecisions. They have created a demand waterfall model with B2B industry average conversion rates at 58%, 49%, and 23% for MQL to SAL to SQL respectively (these figures can and will likely change over time; these are their conversion rate figures as of 2015). **See Figure 2.**

Figure 2 – Demand Waterfall Conversion Rates by SiriusDecisions (as of 2015).

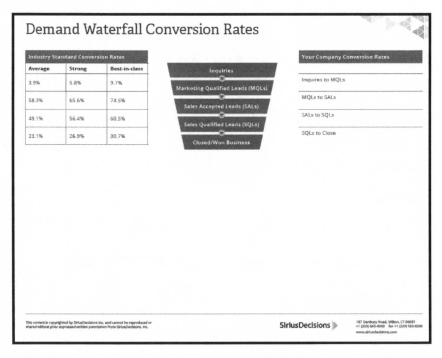

Conversion Rates:

- MQL's (marketing qualified leads) - **58%** conversion
- SAL's (sales accepted leads) - **49%** conversion
- SQL's (sales qualified leads) - **23%** conversion

Over time, and after you've launched some campaigns, you will start to build your own sales funnel conversion rate data. That information can then serve as conversion rate *benchmark* data for future campaigns and you can begin to eliminate third-party data.

HOW TO CALCULATE MARKETING-SOURCED PIPELINE REVENUE: FROM MQL TO SALES OPPORTUNITY

Now, let's take everything that has been discussed in the chapter and look at a real-life example.

Example: Conversion in Action

Start by taking the scenario in which a sales leader is given a $15M overall revenue target for the year. She leads a team of 4 sales reps who sell state-of-the-art IT software to technology buyers within the defense industry. To calculate how many deals she needs to sign to hit her revenue goal, she determines that she needs to close 60 deals given each deal is worth on average $250K in top-line revenue.

Sales Goals:

- Sales goal for number of new deals - **60 Deals**

- Revenue per deal - **$250k**

- Total revenue goal = **$15M**

- **60 Deals * $250k per deal = $15M**

Next, take a $200k annual marketing budget that has been allotted to drive pipeline revenue for her sales team and divide it by an average cost-per-lead of $2k. This comes out to 100 marketing qualified leads that can be expected for her and her team:

- Lead-gen marketing budget - **$200k**

- Average cost-per-lead - **$2k**

- Marketing goal for total number of leads = **100 leads**

- **$200k budget / $2k per lead = 100 leads**

Now, let's take the B2B average conversion rates based on the SiriusDecisions demand waterfall and calculate how many sales opportunities and won deals will come from those 100 marketing-sourced leads. By applying those conversion rates, the 100 marketing qualified leads will turn to 58 sales accepted leads (58% conversion - lead moves from a new status to a working status). Those 58 sales accepted leads then turn to 28 sales qualified leads (49% conversion - lead moves from working status to an opportunity in the pipeline). And, those 28 sales qualified leads then turn to 6 closed-won deals (23% conversion - opportunity moves to a closed-won deal).

Sales Funnel Conversions:

- MQL's = **100 Marketing Qualified Leads**

- SAL's = **58 Sales Accepted Leads (100 * 58% = 58)**

- SQL's = **28 Sales Qualified Leads or $7M in pipeline revenue (58 * 49% = 28)**

- Closed-won = **6 won deals and $1.5M top-line revenue (28 * 23% = 6)**

- ACAC = **$33k (Average Customer Acquisition Cost)**

Those 28 sales opportunities total $7M in marketing-sourced pipeline revenue, and those 6 won deals total $1.5M in marketing-sourced closed revenue ($250k per deal), which equals 10% of the revenue goal for sales that year. Overall, this is a win for the marketing organization given its investment of $200k in this marketing lead-gen campaign.

HOW TO CALCULATE AVERAGE CUSTOMER ACQUISITION COST

$ Budget / # Acquired Clients = $ACAC

One particular metric to take note of in the above example is the ACAC (*Average Customer Acquisition Cost*). This is the marketing cost for securing one new client. In this case the ACAC is $33k. It is calculated by taking the entire marketing budget and dividing it by number of clients acquired or deals won.

$200k / 6 Acquired Clients = $33k ACAC.

HOW TO TRACK MARKETING-INFLUENCED SALES OPPORTUNITES

As referenced in the beginning of this section, *marketing-influenced sales opportunities* are opportunities in the pipeline that marketing influenced after the sales team already generated that opportunity on their own. Whatever the tactic or marketing activity, many opportunities in the pipeline that were generated from the sales team's effort will in some way converge with a marketing campaign/initiative. When this happens, it is critical to track that engagement.

Marketing-influenced sales opportunities is another goal many marketers are measured on, and although not as significant as marketing-sourced sales opportunities, it is still an important part of helping the sales team reach its sales goals, and highlights the value that the marketing team delivers to the organization.

3. Call-to-Action: Document Your Lead & Pipeline Revenue Goals

Now is the time to document your lead and revenue goals, the purpose of which is to build into the rest of your marketing strategy. This will take place specifically in Section 2 (Chapters 4-7) where I will discuss more about how you can embed these lead and revenue goals into your strategy.

Exercise: Document Your Lead & Pipeline Revenue Goals

To begin this process, refer to your Marketing Strategy Working Document, create three columns from left to right and label those columns: *Metrics, Goals,* and *Actuals.* **See Table 3.** For *Metrics,* you should list all of the primary metrics that were discussed in this chapter related to leads, conversion rates, and sourced and influenced percentages. Structure it as so:

Table 3. Define Lead & Revenue Goals

	A	B	C
1	Metrics	Goals	Actuals
2	# of MQL	100	X
3	# of SAL	58	X
4	# of SQL	28	X
5	Total Percentage of Pipeline Revenue Sourced	20%	X
6	Total Percentage of Pipeline Revenue Influenced	30%	X
7			
8			
9			

- **Metrics**

    o # of MQL

- o # of SAL

- o # of SQL

- o Revenue Sourced %

- o Revenue Influenced **%**

- **Goals**

  - o In each row beneath *Goals* list the goal that corresponds to each metric. If your goal is to source 20% of pipeline revenue, then list 20% to that corresponding metric.

- **Actual**

  - o In each row beneath *Actual* list what was actually achieved with respect to that metric. If your goal was to deliver 100 MQL's, but you actually delivered 80 or actually delivered 120, list it as appropriate.

Take note, that you will have your *Actual* figures only once all of your lead-gen campaigns and activities have occurred. Those *Actual* figures should be reported at the end of the year or end of a quarter, when you and other marketing and sales stakeholders review the results of your marketing strategy. These goals and metrics, along with many other KPI's and metrics, will be revisited in Chapter 10 Measure Marketing Performance.

 4. Chapter Bonus Material

Here are some additional best practices and bonus material specific to this chapter:

Customer Lifetime Value:

Average Annual Revenue per Client x Average # of Years Client Remains a Client = Customer Lifetime Value

There is a growing emphasis in many organizations for marketing teams to measure their performance not only through number of MQL's generated, and amount of pipeline revenue sourced or influenced, but also through Customer Lifetime Value or CLV. *Customer Lifetime Value* is defined as the calculated prediction of revenue gained from the future relationship with a client.

CLV is calculated by taking the average annual revenue contributed by clients, multiplied by the average number of years a client remains a client, subtracted by the average customer acquisition cost. Here is how CLV would break down when plugging in some of the figures from the example earlier in the chapter: **$250k average annual revenue x 5 years average - $33k ACAC = $1.22M CLV**. For many marketers, Customer Lifetime Value is the new *ROI (Return on Investment)*.

Learn More about the Sales Approach and Target Accounts

When learning more about sales and revenue goals, it may also be a good idea to learn how the sales team approaches the market in terms of identifying target accounts, specific buyers, and how they generate sales leads. This will equip you with more insights into which accounts you should be targeting, and will help shape your overall strategy.

For example, get a deeper understanding of the account sizes and account characteristics that the sales team is chasing (i.e. if they are targeting primarily net new prospects, up-selling into existing clients, etc). Determine the length of the sales cycle so you can anticipate how long leads and opportunities remain in the sales funnel, and when most buyers are looking to buy. This will pay off dramatically when it comes to crafting the message, creating the content and implementing the media mix! Having a better idea of their sales goals, target accounts character-istics, and sales strategy will result in more confidence as you get ready to execute your strategy.

Calculate Cost-per-Lead Based on Lead Source

Measuring the performance and effectiveness of your marketing strat-egy means measuring *all* of the individual tactical components that make up your strategy. For instance, your lead-gen strategy may be set up so that you are producing leads from many different lead sources: web, events, content campaigns, webinars, etc., therefore the cost-per-lead from each of these disparate campaigns and initiatives will vary (so too will the conversion rates down the funnel). Keep a record of how each of these individual lead-gen activities perform in terms of cost-per-lead and conversion in the sales funnel, so you know whether or not to continue specific marketing tactics. Chapter 10 will provide more detail about measuring and evaluating your strategy once it's in market.

Insider Tips

As I have mentioned throughout the book, **SiriusDecisions** a marketing, product management, and sales consulting firm, and a firm I personally have used in the past, may be a resource in helping you build your lead & revenue goals.

Jason W. Simmons

SECTION 2:
BUILD

Section 2 is centered on *Building,* and includes Chapters 4-7. You will *build* Frameworks for your marketing strategy, specifically a Buyer Persona Framework, Marketing Message Framework, Content Marketing Framework, and Media Mix Framework. These are all important frameworks that ensure your strategy directly aligns with the needs of the buyer in terms of messaging that resonates with them, content they prefer to consume, and channels through which they prefer to consume that content. Once you build all of the required frameworks you will then be ready to advance to Section 3, where you will learn how to *Execute* your marketing strategy.

Chapter 4: Build a buyer persona framework that contains deep insights about your buyers, their preferences, their challenges, the channels where they consume information, and more.

Chapter 5: Build a marketing message framework based on the insights you gained about your buyers from Chapter 4, as well as the information you learned from your stakeholders in Chapter 2, and what you picked up about the market in Chapter 1.

Chapter 6: Build a content marketing framework that aligns with the buyer journey, and which embeds the messaging that was crafted in Chapter 5.

Chapter 7: Build a balanced media mix framework consisting of paid, owned, earned, and social media to deliver to the market all of the content you learned to create from Chapter 6.

CHAPTER 4

BUILDING THE BUYER PERSONA PROFILE

Chapter Overview:

1. Know Your Buyer
2. Using Audience Personas
3. Call-to-Action: Build a Buyer Persona Framework
4. Chapter Bonus Material

Knowing your buyers inside and out is instrumental for a marketing strategy. The insights gained about the buyer (discussed in this chapter) are embedded into the marketing message (discussed in Chapter 5). That message is then embedded into the content strategy (discussed in Chapter 6), and the content is then mapped to a balanced media mix (discussed in Chapter 7). This should help demonstrate why it is so critical to understand your buyers as much as possible before building out other parts of the marketing strategy; because so much of your strategy builds on the insights gained about them.

As you build out your buyer persona profile you will come to learn about two other important audience personas: *Influencers* and *End-users*. For clarification, an influencer is someone who has the ability to affect the decision-making process of your buyer (in most cases it is your buyer's professional colleague). And, an end-user is your buyer's customer or constituent. Where appropriate, document any meaningful findings you come across about these other personas. Although the buyer is the most vital of all audience members, having a better understanding of other audience members will come in handy since you will need to leverage them in your marketing strategy.

In this chapter you will learn how to build a buyer persona framework that provides the most detailed information about your buyers, and you will learn about the importance of embedding other audience personas into your marketing strategy.

1. Know Your Buyer

In order to learn about your buyer, there are some common resources you should tap into. The information you capture there can then be applied to the buyer persona framework—which will be covered in the *Call-to-Action* section at the end of this chapter. There are other resources you can consider to learn about your buyer, however these are the most common and in some cases may be the most accessible to you.

RECOMMENDED RESOURCES

- Focus Groups
- Mrket Research & Buyer Persona Surveys
- Professional Trade Associations
- Client Interviews
- Internal Resources

Focus Groups

Focus groups are one of the most effective methods for capturing meaningful information about your buyers. Focus groups can often be conducted in conjunction with, and as part of, a paid sponsorship with a professional trade association at a regional or national conference. In this scenario, you will likely get to hand pick from a list of current conference attendees who have agreed to participate in the focus group, giving you the benefit of choosing those attendees whose input you would be most interested in hearing.

Here are two critical things to keep in mind when preparing for and conducting a focus group:

1) Determine exactly what it is you hope to learn from this group. You will have a lot of face-to-face time with the focus group, which means that the dialogue that ensues and the feedback that you receive will likely be more valuable than from most other sources. The key here is to prepare as best as possible, and know exactly what it is you wish to learn. The data and insights you will want to learn from this group should include:

- Their work objectives, responsibilities, and goals

- What they consider an ideal market solution, product, or service

- The overall challenges they face in their role and how those challenges can be addressed

- Their views on where they see the market heading and how companies like yours should adapt

- What companies like yours gets right and gets wrong

- Their preferred news or media outlets and where they seek information

- Professional organizations and trade associations they belong to

- Qualities and characteristics they look for in a vendor or company like yours

- Insights and thoughts about your competitors

- Messages or topics that resonate with them

2) Develop a strategy and a plan to get the most out of your focus group. Strategize on how to avoid situations that may lead a focus group into groupthink, or be cognizant of situations where not all feedback is being extracted. For example, if your focus group consists of 10 people but only 5 are actively participating, then perhaps call directly on the less-active members for their input. It could be that they are less vocal than the other members because their voices are being drowned out, so get them more involved.

Another idea for getting thoughtful and articulate input from the group is to play the devil's advocate, or take the other side of an issue to get creative juices flowing in the other direction. Spend some time to think through how you might get the focus group to offer up the most direct, honest, authentic, and unbiased input. And, of course, keep all the questions open-ended and dig deep.

Market Research & Buyer Persona Surveys

There are many firms that specialize in conducting custom market research for organizations that are looking to learn more about their buyers. This research consists of things such as brand analyses and persona surveys, among others. Hiring a market research firm to conduct a persona-based survey can provide you a detailed analysis of your buyer.

These surveys can be focused on a variety of topics—such as how the buyers view your brand and other brands in the market, what challenges and pains they have, their approaches for seeking an industry solution to solve those challenges, and more. If you solicit a firm to conduct these surveys and research, be sure to share with them beforehand the characteristics of the target accounts your organization is actively pursuing. That firm can then target survey participants who work for organizations that match those characteristics. For instance, if you are only pursuing accounts that are public companies, employ 5,000 workers or more, and those which have sales revenue equal to $500M+ annually, then the survey should only target participants who work at organizations that meet those criteria.

Professional Trade Associations

Trade associations were discussed in Chapter 1 as a resource for you to learn about the market landscape. However, trade associations, as you might have already guessed, are also a great way to learn about your buyer. Make a habit of attending on a regular basis the regional and national conferences these associations host.

The conference sessions and dialogue that takes place at these events will provide you a well-rounded view of your buyer and what they are challenged with, as well as what market solutions they may need to help them. Also, trade associations regularly publish new research, findings, and surveys about your buyers and the market. Reviewing those surveys and research will be helpful for you as you build out your buyer persona profile.

Client Interviews

Tapping into existing clients is a convenient way to learn about buyers. However, because they are existing clients means there may be some limitations in terms of input they can offer up—such as describing in detail the challenges they presently face due to lack of a market solution (they are already working with you). Still, they are able to provide valuable insights.

Existing clients can provide feedback about where they feel the market is heading, what future challenges they see for themselves, how organizations like yours should adapt to trends or changes in the market, and what caused them to pursue a market-solution like yours in the first place. Clients are also more than willing to be honest about what your organization is getting wrong and what you can do better.

Internal Resources

You should meet with internal stakeholders to learn about your buyer; this is a resource that is readily at your disposal. The stakeholders you should meet with are the same stakeholders referenced in Chapter 2; sales, product managers, marketers, and other pertinent stakeholders who would know your buyers well.

 # 2. Using Audience Personas

The content in this chapter is about helping you learn not only how to build a buyer persona profile but also about why it is so important for your overall marketing strategy. As you make your way through Chapters 5, 6, and 7, you will learn how to use this buyer persona profile in an actionable way.

Although you are not required to create persona profiles for influencers and end-users, knowing at minimum how to use them and why they are important is critical.

INFLUENCERS

- **Influencer Definition:** Someone who has the ability to affect the decision-making process of your buyer.

Example: Karen the Influencer

Consider the scenario in which a prospective buyer, whom we'll call John and who is a Vice President of Human Resources, has been working closely with one of your sales reps about purchasing a Human Resources Management System (HRMS) to replace his organization's older and outdated HRMS system. A deal appears to be in the works. However, John needs to run the purchase by his colleague, Karen (influencer) who is the Vice President of IT at their organization.

Karen plays somewhat of a significant role in this deal as she is responsible for getting this new HRMS system integrated within the company's network and larger IT infrastructure. She has already let on that she has some concerns related to the amount of time it is going to take to install and integrate with other systems. She's also concerned about the overall time commitment she and her staff will need to devote to providing continuous maintenance for as long as your organization uses this system. She prefers the legacy system your organization already has, because she knows it.

Luckily for you, you anticipated Karen's concerns and objections ahead of time. This is because you took the time to study *influencer personas*. You understand firsthand the role IT influencers play in the decision-making process, what their issues and challenges are, and the potential objections they may have about your HRMS system. You turned this knowledge into action by creating specific marketing content assets specific to IT influencers.

For example, you created several case studies and video testimonials that feature senior-level IT professionals discussing how seamlessly your

HRMS system integrates with other internal IT systems. These IT professionals also reference how much time it saves them on a monthly basis because your system is a much more advanced system compared to older legacy models, and it doesn't require nearly as much ongoing maintenance. Your sales rep and John have a quick meeting about how to alleviate Karen's concerns, and these content assets are the first things that come to your sales rep's mind.

After John and your sales rep have more dialogue with Karen and after sharing these content assets with her so that she can learn first-hand what other IT professionals had to say about your HRMS system, she agrees to work collaboratively with them on integrating and supporting this new HRMS system. It's a win for everyone!

Had you not taken the effort to learn more about your influencers and put forth the effort to address them in your marketing strategy, then those content assets would have never been created and available to Karen. Thus, her concerns and reservations may not have been fully addressed and the deal may have never gone through.

END-USERS

- **End-User Definition:** Your buyer's customer / constituent

Example: The Hospital Patient End-User

Unlike influencers the end-users do not need to be marketed to directly as they do not play a direct role in the decision-making process of a purchase, therefore their approval isn't required. However, this persona is extremely valuable to your buyers since that is their main customer. For context and clarification, here are some examples of buyers and end-users: If you sell healthcare products or services to Hospitals CEOs and executives, then the end-user would be hospital patients. Likewise, if you sell education products or services to University Deans and Presidents, then the end-user would be college students.

Day in and day out your buyers are constantly working toward providing a better experience for their customer (in your case, the end-user). In fact, it's probably safe to say that the bulk of their professional working-life revolves around nothing but their customer experience. Given these strong connections of your buyers and end-users means there is a ripe opportunity to embed these end-user personas into your marketing strategy.

You can achieve this through a common marketing tactic called *story-telling marketing*. Story-telling simply means developing messaging and content that puts the end-user at the center of a story. Using the previous example, if hospital CEOs and executives are your buyers, perhaps developing a story around *a patient's road to recovery* may make for good story-telling. The story could be about the patient experience—from heartbreaking diagnosis to miraculous road to recovery, all the while it was your solution that helped make the recovery possible.

The real advantage of storytelling marketing is that it humanizes your brand and can evoke positive, visceral, and emotional reactions from your buyers by showing the impact your solution has on the lives of their customers. Story-telling will help buyers visualize the deeper and more meaningful experience they could be having on their customers' lives through the use of your solution.

Diversifying your marketing strategy to include story-telling marketing can be extremely powerful because the message is centered on how an end-user's life has been touched, changed, or simply made better through your solution. It is a potent form of marketing. Examples of story-telling marketing content include video testimonials, stories, and blogs written by end-users.

BUYERS

The beginning of this chapter discusses how the buyer persona profile is used to help develop other parts of your overall marketing strategy. Insights gained about the buyer are then used to help develop the marketing message, that message is embedded into the marketing content, and that content is then distributed to the market via the buyers' preferred media channels.

Example: John the Buyer

To help you visualize that process, think about the scenario used in the *influencer* example. In this example it was John, VP of Human Resources who was the buyer. Applying the same methods used in the previous example, let's say you've learned everything there is to know about VP's of Human Resources because you took the time to build out a buyer persona profile. Those insights then informed and helped you craft a message specific to the issues, challenges, and desires facing that type of buyer. Your messaging framework directly aligns with everything that they care about.

You take your well-crafted message and begin developing various content assets that Human Resources buyers such as John have indicated they prefer to consume. You develop these unique and specific content assets for each phase within the buyer journey (the buyer's journey is covered in Chapter 6). You know through your buyer persona research which types of content Human Resource professionals prefer to read, such as blogs and white papers.

You also know that buyers like John prefer topics related to how the HR business role is steadily evolving and how the HR function plays a significant part in employee retention and satisfaction at organizations— those are topics that John really cares about. You know this because you conducted a focus group with several HR professionals who overwhelmingly highlighted employee retention as a subject that they were most eager to explore. It was also validated through other resources when researching about Human Resource buyers. So, you make sure that employee retention and satisfaction are the key topics discussed in your content strategy.

That content is then distributed to various media channels. Those media channels are specific to the channels VP's of Human Resources prefer and trust. For instance, there are two specific HR industry trade outlets that VP's flock to and read more than any other. You know this due to your research.

Because of that, you decide that one of your many marketing tactics to attract these buyers will be to heavily advertise on those trade outlets. In addition to advertising via those outlets, you also work with the publication editors of those two outlets to secure guest-blogs and sponsored op-eds so that your company's content is featured on their sites, and, thus, are certain to be read and consumed by your key buyer.

All of this happened because you knew your buyer's interests, preferences, challenges, and needs.

▶ 3. Call-to-Action: Build a Buyer Persona Framework

Once you have a deeper understanding of your buyer you can then begin to build the Buyer Persona Framework. The purpose of this framework is to capture deep insights about your buyer that will allow you to better understand them, know how to build a message that resonates with them, and where and how to market to them. The Buyer Persona Framework in particular helps to anchor the other frameworks you will learn about and create in the next three chapters: the Messaging Framework, the Content Framework, and the Media Mix Framework.

Once complete, the structure of this Buyer Persona Framework will serve as a living document, and can be referenced whenever needed. The content within the framework will need to be updated regularly as the solution, market, organization, and buyer changes and evolves over time. Make plans to keep this document up-to-date to reflect any changes and keep it timely and relevant.

Exercise: Build a Buyer Persona Framework

To build the framework, and using your Marketing Strategy Working Document, begin creating a list of Buyer Insights (below). Start with just one column, and label it *Buyer Persona Profile*. Under that column, list each Buyer Insight, one by one. To the right of each Buyer Insight, fill it in with the appropriate information you have collected through your research. **See Table 4.**

Table 4. Buyer Persona Framework

	A	S
1		BUYER PERSONA PROFILE
2	Robust Buyer Description	
3	Buyer Objectives	
4	Buyer Challenges	
5	Current Industry/Market Issues	
6	Buyer Goals	
7	Buyer Concerns about market solutions	
8	Buyer key buzzwords	
9	Messaging takeaways	
10	Where buyers consume information (media, news outlets, trade publications, social media etc)	

It's always better to build out the Buyer Persona Framework with more information, data, and content than what's typically needed, this way you can trim down and edit the document as you refine and then finalize it. **See Figure 3** for how you might represent key insights of your buyer persona profile on a presentation slide.

Figure 3. Buyer Persona Profile on Presentation Slide

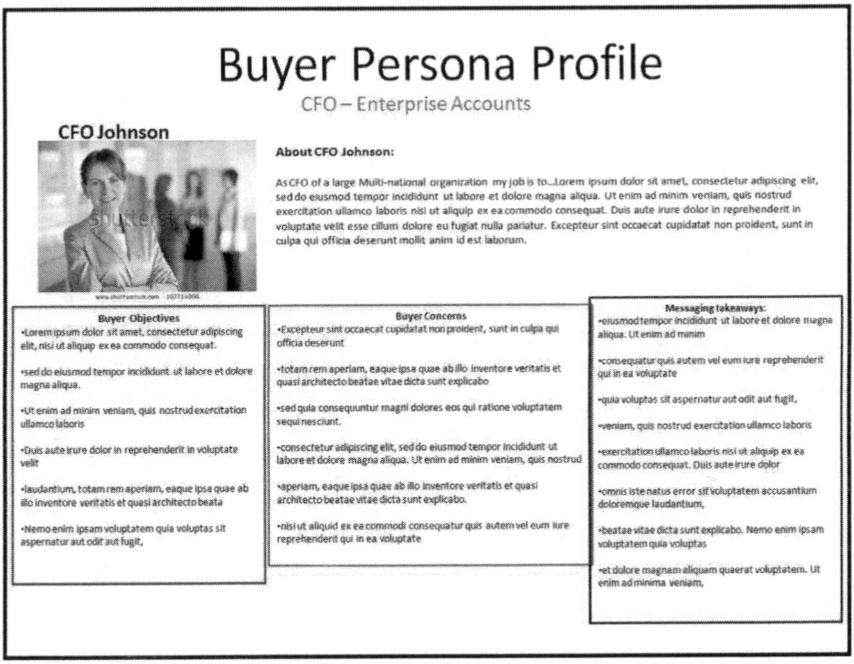

The buyer insights in your Framework should include:

- Robust Buyer Description

- Buyer Objectives

- Buyer Challenges

- Current Industry & Market Issues

- Buyer Goals

- Buyer Concerns About Market Solutions

- Buyer Key Buzzwords

- Messaging Takeaways

- Where buyers consume information: media channels, social media, news, and industry trades

The list of insights above are common and should be a good starting point in order to provide you the broad information you need to know about your buyer. You're welcome to add more insights to this list, remove some insights on this list, or simply change it altogether. For example, you could add a *Demographics* insight as part of the template, and capture information such as age, race, gender, and geographic data. Segmenting your buyers this way could provide inferences to help you better understand their preferences on media channels, how they like to consume information, and where they like to consume information. Take some time to develop these profile insights and, if needed, look to external resources that specialize in building buyer profiles and personas.

4. Chapter Bonus Material

Here are some additional best practices and bonus material specific to this chapter:

Insider Tips

There are many external resources including blogs, articles, and books that could help you build robust persona frameworks. Some of the most notable figures and thought-leaders on the subject of buyer personas, and whom I personally follow on social media to help me with my own efforts, are **Tony Zambito** and **Ardath Albee**. Both have written extensively about this topic and currently help organizations build their own buyer persona and content strategies.

CHAPTER 5
CRAFTING THE MESSAGE

Chapter Overview:

1. Capture All Viewpoints
2. Understand Messaging Core Elements
3. Call-to-Action: Craft a Marketing Message Framework
4. Chapter Bonus Material

By now you should have everything you need to start crafting a compelling, competitive, and winning message for the market. Take a moment to review all that you've accomplished on your journey to create a marketing strategy. You have completely engrossed yourself with the market environment, the priorities of business stakeholders, the buyers, and other key audience members. This new knowledge you have acquired provides you all the key ingredients necessary to put together a framework for a winning marketing message.

This marketing message framework will help to guarantee that all the marketing content you create and deploy out into the market accurately addresses the desires, challenges, and needs of buyers. That message will be embedded into each content asset you create, regardless of type—whether it is a blog, case study, video testimonial, or white paper. The content will harness the core elements of the marketing message framework. In the next chapter (Chapter 6) I will more thoroughly discuss how you can put together a thoughtful content marketing strategy.

In this chapter, you will learn how to craft a marketing message framework which is made up of several core elements, and which takes into consideration all that you have learned about your buyer, the market, and the priorities of your stakeholders.

1. Capture all Viewpoints

Before you begin detailing the value propositions, positioning statements, and campaign themes you should first consider the viewpoints of three key stakeholders, or groups. Look at the framework through the prism of the market and competitive landscape (discussed in Chapter 1) internal stakeholders (discussed in Chapter 2) and buyers (discussed in Chapter 4). Use these three viewpoints as a guide when you begin building out the marketing messaging framework. A blog post written by Jenna Hanington at Pardot, accurately captures the viewpoints or angles that a marketer needs to take into account when creating a messaging framework (Hanington, 2015).

a) **Competitive/Market Viewpoint:** Having a strong pulse on what's happening in the market and how your competitors are positioning themselves will help you develop a message that is unique and differentiated. For instance, in a saturated market full of competitors, you want to make sure that your message and value proposition doesn't blend in and get lost with the others. Think about how you can go to market with a differentiated, eye-catching message that will help you get noticed and stand apart from everyone else.

b) **Internal Stakeholder Viewpoint:** Take into account the ideas and perspectives you gathered from your internal stakeholders, specifically the sales team, on how your company's solution could be better positioned in the market. They have shared with you their strategic priorities, as referenced in Chapter 2, and the marketing message was likely a topic of discussion. The sales team is in the best position to give feedback about which messages resonate and which don't when they are meeting with prospects.

c) **Buyer Viewpoint:** The knowledge you acquired in Chapter 4 through the building of a Buyer Persona Framework will have prepared you to create a message with the buyer in mind. Through that research you have learned about your buyers' concerns, the issues that keep them up at night, and what they are seeking in a solution to help them solve their problems. Armed with this information, you are then able to develop a message that resonates with them and addresses their struggles head on.

See Figure 4 for an example of a marketing message framework developed by HighFive.

Figure 4. Marketing Message Framework (Developed by HighFive at highfive.com)

BRAND PROMISE	Video conferencing you can actually love.		
POSITIONING STATEMENT	Highfive is the first video conferencing product designed to connect every employee and every conference room in your entire company.		
TARGET AUDIENCE	1) C-level Executive (influencer), 2) Director of IT (buyer), and 3) End-User (user)		
MISSION	Our mission is to make every conversation face-to-face.		
TONE OF VOICE	Empowering, progressive, human, and cheeky.		
ELEVATOR PITCH	Highfive is video conferencing you can actually love. We believe teams work best face-to-face. That's why we designed the first video conferencing product designed to connect every person and room in an organization. Highfive provides an all-in-one video conferencing hardware device that plugs into any TV screen, turning any ordinary meeting room into a video room. Highfive also provides cloud apps, which allow employees and guests to simply click a link from any laptop or mobile device and instantly connect face-to-face with anyone, anywhere. The hardware device costs the same as a high-end iPad and the cloud apps are free. We think video shouldn't be a boardroom luxury – it should be available everywhere.		
BRAND PILLARS	Easy	Everywhere	Enterprise
HEADLINE BENEFITS	Highfive is beautifully simple video conferencing you can start or join with a single click.	Twenty conference rooms for the price of one Cisco or Polycom system.	Built for businesses, not social networking.
SUPPORTING EXAMPLES	• Join calls from your calendar, SMS, or email by clicking a URL • Hand off video calls from your personal device to a meeting room TV with a swipe or click – no remote control needed. • 5-min plug and play setup	• Comparable systems cost ~$15k per room • At the price of an iPad, Highfive can be deployed in every room • Free apps let people stay connected at their desks or on the go	• Must sign up with work email address • Domain-based security model • Enterprise reliability and security built by the same people that built Google Apps for Business

▶ 2. Understand Messaging Core Elements

The messaging framework is made up of several core elements, which are broken into two categories: *solution specific* core elements and *brand specific* core elements. These two categories are as straight-forward as it sounds. Solution specific core elements will be messaging specific to your solution, product, or service and the brand specific core elements will be messaging specific to your company and brand.

Let's take a look at some common core elements, and as you read through these, visualize how you could use them in your marketing message.

SOLUTION SPECIFIC CORE ELEMENTS

- **Buyer Audience**

  - Create a list of the buyer persona titles your solutions targets.

  - For instance, if you sell into senior-level Finance professionals, your buyers may include:

    » Chief Accounting Officers

    » Chief Financial Officers

    » Senior Vice Presidents of Finance

    » Vice Presidents of Finance

- **Buyer Buzzwords**

  - The buyer persona research you collected from Chapter 4 will likely be rich in buzzwords. These are specific words and nomenclature that are related to the buyer's industry or buyer's job title.

  - Reflect back on surveys, focus groups, and industry analysts' reports to see which buzzwords are consistently used. You can then strategically embed these keywords into your message and marketing content. This will validate to your audience that you understand the industry and the nuances within—and that you speak their language.

- **Problem(s) This Solution Solves**

  - Think of 2 or 3 problems this solution solves for your buyers, or more. This could be things like *Improves operational efficiencies by eliminating duplicative processes* or *Improves top of line revenue by finding and opening up new streams of revenue.* Be sure the problems are very specific to your solution.

- o This core element is particularly helpful as it will demonstrate to your buyer how your solution helps to solve their problem. Addressing the problems your solutions solves should be included in almost every content asset you send out to the market, whether it is directly laid out or mentioned tacitly.

- **Value Proposition**

  - o Peep Laja, Founder of Conversion XL has an excellent value proposition definition that is worth using here. In one of his blogs, he states that "A *value proposition* is a promise of value to be delivered. It's the primary reason a prospect should buy from you. In a nutshell, a value proposition is a clear statement that:

    - » explains how your product solves customers' problems or improves their situation (relevancy),

    - » delivers specific benefits (quantified value),

    - » tells the ideal customer why they should buy from you and not from the competition (unique differentiation)." (Laja, No Published Date Provided)

  - o Apply the Peep Laja approach to building out your value propositions.

- **Positioning Statement**

  - o The *positioning statement* is a short but simple statement that best describes your solution to the market while differentiating you from competitors and highlighting its value. Look at it this way—if you had just a few seconds to briefly and succinctly explain what your solution is to the market or a prospect how would you explain it? Think of this as an elevator pitch to the market.

- o These positioning statements can best be used at the tail-end of any content asset; blog, white paper, case study, eBook, video asset, etc. The positioning statement is best used as a coda or summation in marketing assets as a reminder of why your solution is the best.

- **Campaign Theme**

  - o The *campaign theme* is a specific message to the market that tells a story about how your solution helps buyers and is of value to the market. It can tell this story in a creative, fun, innovative, or imaginative way.

  - o The campaign theme should be a unique message and one that is germane to the market.

  - o All of the marketing content you create for your marketing strategy should center on this one theme.

  - o An example of a campaign theme within the healthcare industry may simply be *Building Tomorrow's Healthcare Infrastructure*.

The content strategy, which is discussed in Chapter 6, will detail more closely how the campaign message and theme comes to life through content.

BRAND SPECIFIC CORE ELEMENTS

If you are already working for an organization, as opposed to just starting your own business, then you likely already have a set of brand language guidelines your company uses. These guidelines describe and define your brand, and how your brand is represented in the market via print, digital, and broadcast media. It is a standard set of guidelines used across the entire organization.

These brand specific core elements are already established and will be used anytime your organization has a message that is visible and intended for the market. Below are common core elements that are found within most organizations' *brand guidelines*.

If you are not familiar with your company's brand language guidelines, I highly recommend you become familiar with these so you better understand how your company views itself and how it positions itself in the market.

- **Tagline**

    o The *tagline* represents your brand more so than the solution you are selling, it projects what you do (even if not directly) while leaving a lasting impression.

    o Examples of most well-known taglines include Nike's: *Just do it* or Apple Inc's: *Think different.*

- **Brand Promise**

    o The brand promise is not the same as the tagline. The tagline is catchy whereas the brand promise is inspirational and up-lifting. It connects emotionally with clients.

    o Brand-promises are not used directly in marketing campaigns. It is meant to serve as the creed or brand philosophy for the organization, which is then felt by the market indirectly.

- Some well-known brand promises include Coca Cola's: *To inspire moments of optimism and uplift.* Or Nike's: *To bring inspiration and innovation to every athlete in the world.*

- **Mission**

  - A mission statement is a tangible, action-oriented goal your organization is pursuing. It is usually brief, simple, and concise; and it explains how it seeks to help the organization's customers, employees, and owners.

  - A good mission statement to refer to is one by Patagonia, which states: *Build the best product, cause no unnecessary harm, use business to inspire and implement solutions to the environmental crisis.*

- **Vision**

  - The vision is transformative. Whereas the mission statement is specific, tangible, and describes what your organization is trying to achieve; the vision is philosophical and broad. It outlines where the company is heading, what it wants to be, and the positive impact it hopes to have on its clients and/or industry.

  - A good example of a vision statement comes from Amazon: *To be earth's most customer-centric company, where customers can find and discover anything they might want to buy online.*

- **Tone-of-Voice**

o The *tone-of-voice* is how you intend for your message to come across and be interpreted by consumers of your content. It conveys feeling.

o Tone-of-voice is often times defined just using one-word adjectives; for example: helpful, conversational, optimistic, forward-thinking.

▶ 3. Call-to-Action: Craft a Marketing Message Framework

The purpose of the Marketing Message Framework is to serve as the cornerstone for each content asset you produce, and it should be referenced prior to producing each asset. This will ensure that all your content has embedded within it your core marketing message.

For instance, let's say you will soon be writing an eBook that demonstrates thought-leadership; before you put pen to paper or keyboard to word document, you should refer to your messaging framework as a guide to help you through that writing process and to keep you on track with the message.

Exercise: Craft a Marketing Message Framework

Begin categorizing your notes from the work you completed in Chapters 1-4. Your objective is to identify the notes that you believe are critical to helping you craft your *core elements*. This could be key information you picked up when meeting with internal stakeholders, what you learned when conducting research about the market environment and competitors, and what you gathered from the buyer persona research work you conducted.

As you read through and filter those notes, begin matching the most salient nuggets of information and data you find to the core elements of your marketing message such as *value proposition, position state-ment,* and all the others. For example, let's say you learned through your buyer persona research that your buyers have a very favorable view of your brand. In fact, it is something you came across frequently during your research. That would then be an excellent opportunity to make that brand favorability, trust, and reputation part of your *value proposition's* core element.

Another example may be where you came across certain industry jargon or keywords when learning about the market (Chapter 1) or researching your buyers (Chapter 4), you can then add that jargon to your *buyer buzzwords* core element. This will come in handy when you begin to strategically place those buyer buzzwords into your content thereby establishing further credibility with your buyers.

Similar to the Buyer Persona Framework in the previous chapter, your Marketing Message Framework will be a living document that can be referenced whenever needed. The content within the framework will need to be updated regularly as internal and external forces influence your marketing message strategy. Such as, changes in the buyer prefer-ences, changes to the solution, or shifts in the marketplace. Make plans to keep this document up-to-date to reflect any changes and keep it timely and relevant.

Use the Marketing Strategy Working Document to begin compiling a list of the core elements you want to build upon for your strategy. Start with just one column, labeling it *Marketing Message Framework* and under-neath that label and header begin to list the core elements one by one. To the right of each core element, begin filling it out with the applicable information you have gleaned. **See Table 5.**

Table 5. Marketing Message Framework

	MARKETING MESSAGE FRAMEWORK:
Buyer Audience: (solution specific)	
Buyer Buzzwords: (solution specific)	
Problem(s) the solution solves (solution specific)	
Value Proposition (solution specific)	
Positioning Statement (solution specific)	
Campaign Theme (solution specific)	
Tagline (brand specific)	
Brand Promise (brand specific)	
Mission (brand specific)	
Vision (brand specific)	
Tone-of-voice (brand specific)	

Here are the core elements you should start with:

- **Buyer Audience**

- **Buyer Buzzwords**

- **Problems This Solution Solves**

- **Value Propositions**

- **Positioning Statement**

- **Campaign Theme**

- **Tagline**

- **Brand Promise**

- **Mission**

- **Vision**

- **Tone-of-Voice**

As a final tip here, and as was mentioned in the previous chapter, it's always easier to start with more information and then trim down from there, rather than starting with too little information and trying to add to it later. Include more information first, and then whittle away the unnecessary items as you work through each core element. You will soon end up with a polished, refined—and most importantly—thoughtful marketing message framework.

4. Chapter Bonus Material

Here are some additional best practices and bonus material specific to this chapter:

Align to Brand Guidelines

As you work on building your Marketing Message Framework, make sure that you refer to and align it with your organization's brand language guidelines. These brand guidelines create a standard for how all of your organization's products, solutions, and services are positioned in the market. These guidelines were discussed earlier in the chapter, but are worth mentioning here as it is important to frequently reference those guidelines when building out messaging and content.

Insider Tips

To help you better build a messaging framework here are a couple of common industry resources I have found useful for me, personally, as a marketer, and that you may find useful too. Organizations such as **Pragmatic Marketing,** which specialize in helping organizations build their marketing message, could be a valuable resource that will help you build a powerful marketing message. As was noted earlier the book, **SiriusDecisions,** a B2B marketing, sales, and product management consulting firm, is another valuable external resource to consider when building a marketing message.

CHAPTER 6
CREATING THE CONTENT

Chapter Overview:

1. Understand the Buyer's Journey
2. Align Content to the Buyer's Journey
3. Center Content on the Message
4. Call-to-Action: Create a Content Marketing Framework
5. Chapter Bonus Material

There's a common phrase in the content marketing world: **content is king**. Most any marketer would agree that that is true—content is king. Having a thoughtful content strategy is one of the most consequential components within the entire marketing strategy. Look at content as the medium to deliver a powerful message, through every phase of the buyer's journey, about how your solution can help make people's lives better.

Content is the medium that allows you to elevate your offering as the leading solution to help solve your buyers' problems. It is the medium through which you are able to creatively and artfully articulate the challenges facing the market, to have a perspective on the market, and to propose meaningful solutions.

Some might argue that the entire marketing strategy hinges on one thing alone—a thoughtful and sophisticated content strategy. And, most would agree because it is the buyer alone who is the ultimate decider on whether or not what you say, when you say it, and the way you say it is of any value to them. Once content has been deployed in the market it is completely out of your hands, its efficacy and relevancy is determined by those who consume it.

In this chapter you will learn how to build a Content Marketing Framework that maps content to the buyer's journey and that aligns your content strategy to the elements within your Marketing Message Framework.

▶ 1. Understand the Buyer's Journey

The buyer's journey is the path one travels when making a purchasing decision. Different types of content are needed to accommodate the buyer through each buying phase of the journey, and to help them seamlessly transition from one phase to the next.

Generally speaking, there are **three specific phases** that buyers encounter in the journey before the actual purchase takes place. These phases are: *awareness phase, consideration phase, and decision phase.* (Note: there are many versions of the buyer journey, but this three-phase journey is the most recognized within the B2B marketing community). These phases are also commonly referred to *top-of-funnel*, middle-of-funnel, and bottom-of-funnel, respectively, if you instead prefer to look at the journey as a funnel one passes through.

I will use a generic example of the B2B buyer journey to best articulate how one would pass through it.

Example: Jane Moves through the Buyer's Journey

AWARENESS: A prospective buyer whom I'll call Jane is in the market for a solution; in an effort to educate herself more about her work challenges and problems, and about which solutions may exist, she begins to do some preliminary research online. In doing so she stumbles across a blog that was co-authored by one of your organization's internal stakeholders and an existing client. It is a thought-leadership content piece about how buyers such as Jane can implement certain solutions and best practices that make their job easier; those best practices indirectly and tacitly tie back to your offering/solution. In fact, within the blog there is a hyperlink to a landing page that contains a gated white paper (gated = requires form submission). The white paper is more of a "how-to" guide that helps buyers better understand their problem and learn how different solutions could help them. Jane downloads the white paper, reads it, and continues to broaden her research until she feels fully educated on this topic.

CONSIDERATION: Jane now begins to receive periodic emails from your organization. Her contact info was captured via the white paper form and now an automated email *nurture campaign* is underway. These emails contain case studies, video testimonials, fact-sheets, and other content, which offer deeper insights about the nuts and bolts of your solution and how it is helping others such as Jane solve problems. Jane reads the emails, case studies, and other content, and begins to visit your website to learn even more. In fact, she begins to narrow her search down to specific brands and solutions which she may purchase.

DECISION: Jane is active in the nurture campaign and your *marketing automation system* is reporting her activity such as click-throughs, page-views and other engagements. A trigger is set and you are notified that Jane has reached a certain level of activity in your campaign. An inside sales rep views her engagement history within the campaign and is able to see exactly what content she has been exposed to, and with which she has consumed. This inside sales rep reaches out to Jane to gauge her interest and qualify her as a lead (see Chapter 3 on BANT qualification). Upon qualification the rep sets up an in-person meeting or phone call with Jane and with the territory sales rep for a personalized demo and deeper discussion of your solution. The sales rep speaks with her and then invites her to an upcoming event your company is hosting specifically for buyers in the sales pipeline such as Jane.

In this example, a number of content assets were used to help Jane move through the buyer's journey. For each phase within the journey the content was designed specifically for that phase. A well thought-out content strategy will help move Jane along in her buying decision. The content types in this example included white papers, blogs, case studies, video testimonials, a company website with specific landing page, a personalized demo, and a company-hosted event.

▶ 2. Align Content to the Buyer's Journey

Now that you've just finished reading about Jane's experience, from the previous example, it's time to take a closer look at how and why certain content assets align to different phases within the buyer journey.

Awareness Content

Content in the awareness phase is about one thing: building trust and credibility with the buyer. This is especially crucial if you are a new entrant into the market, or are operating in a newly formed market and need to establish your presence. Trust is built by showing that you have a perspective, which is seen as credible and valuable, about how buyers can solve their problems by using specific solutions or best-practices.

Trust and credibility are paramount to the buyer's journey because these buyers are still in the awareness phase. As they are educating themselves on their challenges, the content that is most effective would be what is called **prescriptive content** or **how-to-content**. This is content that helps buyers better understand how to solve their problems.

For instance, if you recently decided you were going to lose weight, you would most likely be interested in content, articles, or blogs that tell you what steps you can take with respect to diet and exercise that will help you shed pounds and look your best. Here, the problem is how to lose weight, and the content that helps you solve that is content that provides guidance, instructions, and advice on how to accomplish the goal of losing weight.

Here's another example that's specific to B2B. Let's say you sell security hardware and software to VP's of Security who oversee large facilities or complexes. Now that you know there are three phases to the buyer's journey, you might contemplate writing a blog or white paper on a subject titled *5 Ways to Keep Facilities Safe from Burglary,* which would be geared specifically for prospective buyers who are currently in the awareness phase. A content piece on this subject will likely be of strong interest to a VP of Security who wants to explore new approaches on how to keep those facilities protected because he/she has a strong desire to ensure their facilities are safe from crime.

Also, notice that the title for this content piece has absolutely nothing to do with your solution, rather it has everything to do with preventing crime at large-scale facilities and complexes. This is an excellent example of *awareness* content as it directly addresses a buyer's concern and details helpful tips to solve their problems; most significantly it builds trust and credibility by demonstrating your competence and expertise on this subject.

What's most important about awareness phase content is that it should *not* be about you. It should be about the problem itself. By establishing your expertise in this area, you are establishing trust with your core audience. Your buyers are not ready for a sales pitch during the awareness phase, so don't give it to them here. However, the way you frame your messaging in the awareness phase should ultimately serve to support and strengthen your offering or solution.

For big awareness pieces such as surveys, research reports, eBooks, and white papers, you should favor gating that content (requiring a form submission to access that content). This is so that you can place those who download that content on email nurture campaigns where they will continue to get exposure to content farther down the funnel. Smaller awareness pieces such as blogs, infographics, and others need not be gated.

- **Common Awareness Content Types:**
  - White Papers
  - eBooks
  - Blogs
  - Surveys
  - Thought-leadership webinars & podcasts
  - Press releases
  - Infographics
  - Conference sessions presentations

Consideration Content

Unlike awareness phase content in which the primary objective is about building trust by establishing your expertise, the consideration phase content should primarily be about you. Now that buyers have been educated through the awareness phase content, and now that you have gained their trust, it is time to tell them a little bit more about your offering. This is the phase where content assets like case studies, video testimonials, your website, and sales-sheets will come in handy.

Case studies and any other *earned media* are most significant here. Showcasing how your existing clients are benefiting from your solution is highly valuable to prospects because it allows them to visualize how your solution could be applied to their unique situation. It can also help them determine what those outcomes may look like as well.

- **Common Consideration Content Types:**

    o Case studies

    o Company website & landing pages

    o Sales sheets

    o Video Testimonials

    o Solution-oriented webinars & podcasts

Decision Content

Content in this phase is where the rubber meets the road; consider for a moment you are shopping for a car and are going through your own buyer's journey—you read reputable car review websites like *Car and Driver, Kelly Blue Book, Edmunds* and similar publications. You read blogs written by those who test-drove different vehicles. You then narrow your search to a couple of car manufacturers and begin to review their websites to learn more about the specific car models and car specs. You are now ready for a test-drive; the test-drive in this case is the *decision-content* asset here. You are getting the opportunity to experience your potential purchase.

As buyers for your solution move to the last stage of the buyer journey, you should come up with some creative ideas that afford them an opportunity to test-drive your solution. Perhaps this is a customized demo for their organization, or perhaps it is a trial offer in which they can use your solution for a short period of time to see if it's the right solution for them.

Another successful content type for this phase includes small in-person events. As an example, an event such as a one-day forum or summit that brings together thought-leaders, other industry leaders, and your prospective buyers can be powerful (this was briefly mentioned in Chapter 2). It can be powerful because the experience and dialogue that unfolds at these events can help to elevate your brand, establish your credibility, and differentiate you from the competition.

Whatever your ideas for decision-phase content, the goal here is to give prospects an up close and personal look at your company, brand, or offering and help them visualize what that partnership with you might look like.

- **Common Decision Content Types:**

  - Company hosted events

  - Demo's

  - Assessments

  - On-site presentations

See Figure 5 for how marketing content should align with the buyer journey.

Figure 5. Content Aligned with the Buyer Journey

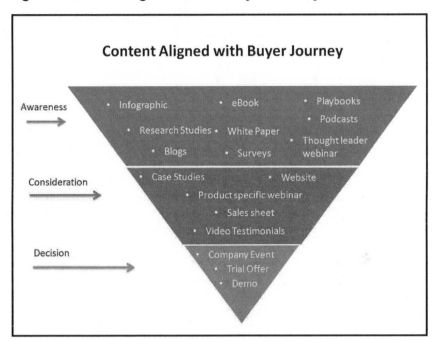

▶ 3. Center Content on the Message

Now that you have a better idea of the buyer's journey and are ready to start creating content, you need to make certain your content is centered on the Marketing Message Framework you developed from Chapter 5. The purpose of centering your content on that framework is to create consistency and clarity about the message you are trying to convey. Look at the Marketing Message Framework as a roadmap on how to construct the message that will live inside your content.

Apply the Marketing Message Framework

Before developing each individual content piece, review the Marketing Message Framework for things like tone-of-voice, brand promise, and value propositions. This will serve as a quick refresher of your core elements and help to reinforce how to use them. As was emphasized, the Marketing Message Framework was largely built on the buyer persona profile, and that profile is rooted in data and research about the challenges and needs your buyers are facing in the market every day. Thus, reviewing the Marketing Message Framework before creating each content asset helps to ensure your content is pertinent and that it accurately articulates the challenges buyers are facing in the market.

Lastly, the Marketing Message Framework should be applied differently to each content type, whether it is a white paper, blog, case study, or sales-sheet. For example, a value proposition in a white paper may be positioned or worded differently than it is in a sales-sheet; and reviewing the Marketing Message Framework before creating your content assets may help you think more critically about how to embed those core elements specific to the content type and its place in the buyer's journey.

Incorporate Campaign Theme

Within the Marketing Message Framework is your campaign theme. Of all the core elements in your Marketing Message Framework, this one will be the most visible to the consumers of your content as it is your front-and-center message to the market. Make sure that your campaign theme is the central message in each content asset. Using the same example from the previous chapter, if your campaign theme is *Building Tomorrow's Healthcare Infrastructure*, then each content piece should be centered on that message.

Perhaps a video testimonial featuring a client discussing how your organization helped them transform their healthcare infrastructure, or a blog written by one of your executives provides thought-leadership about the need for healthcare companies to invest in infrastructure to improve patient healthcare. A content strategy, in which every content asset is connected to one central campaign theme provides your buyer with deeper clarity of your offering, a better understanding how you can help them solve their problems, and a more positive view of your company, brand, and solution. A content strategy that has a disjointed messaging strategy, in which content assets are not connected to either a campaign theme or where the message is inconsistent, can have adverse effects.

▶ 4. Call-to-Action: Create a Content Marketing Framework

The purpose of the Content Marketing Framework is to map your content strategy to the buyer's journey and to help you stay organized as you plan, build, and publish content for the market. Your Content Marketing Framework should consist of two separate items: A List of Mapped Content, and an Editorial Calendar.

Exercise: Create a Content Marketing Framework

1) A List of Mapped Content: Using your Marketing Strategy Working Document, create three columns to represent each of the three phases of the buyer's journey: *awareness, consideration, decision.* **See Table 6.** In each column, under each phase, list the content assets that you currently have and any that you may need to create for your content strategy and that align to each phase. For instance, in the Awareness Phase column, list the content that you currently have or that you need to create such as white papers, infographics, podcasts, or blogs. Repeat the process for Consideration Phase and Decision Phase. The *editorial calendar*, which is discussed next, will be a separate document.

Table 6. Content Mapped to Buyer Journey

	A	B	C
1	Top of Funnel Content (AWARENESS)	Middle of Funnel Content (CONSIDERATION)	Bottom of Funnel Content (DECISION)
2	White Paper	Case Studies	Demo's
3	Blogs	Video Testimonials	Evaluations
4	Surveys	Sales-Sheets	Company-hosted events
5	Thought-leadership webinars & podcasts	FAQ's	
6	Infographics	Solution-oriented webinars & podcasts	
7		Website & Landing pages	
8			
9			
10			
11	CONTENT SHOULD BE CENTERED ON CAMPAIGN THEME		
12	OPTIMIZE CONTENT FOR SEARCH		
13	CALLS TO ACTION REQUIRED FOR ALL CONTENT		
14	TURN TO YOUR EDITORIAL CALENDAR FOR TIMING OF CREATING AND PUBLISHING CONTENT		

2) An Editorial Calendar: In a separate spreadsheet, create twelve tabs to correspond with each month of the year (Microsoft Excel® has pre-loaded templates you can use to create the calendar format). The editorial calendar will help you organize, plan, develop, and publish content over a one-year time frame (or choose your own timeframe). This also affords you the opportunity to align your content strategy with the buying and sales cycles of the market, which, in turn, helps to ensure your content marketing strategy is indeed strategic. It also allows you to view your content strategy in an overarching way so that you can see how everything fits together. Not using an editorial calendar as part of your content marketing strategy can lead to disjointed and unbalanced publishing of individual content assets with no real vision for how each piece of content is connected to a larger strategy.

Determine how far in advance your editorial calendars needs to be up-to-date, whether it's 3 months, 6 months, 9 months or 12 months. Once you have a better idea on the timeline, think about how all of your content will be interconnected. For example if you are planning a company-hosted event for prospective clients in the month of September, it may not be a bad idea to launch and promote a new white paper in April, several months prior to that event. Those who download the whitepaper are then engaged through a nurture campaign path and likely to become strong prospects who will attend that event.

As with the Marketing Message Framework and Buyer Persona Framework in the previous chapters, the Content Marketing Framework will be a living document that can be referenced whenever needed. However, it will need to be updated regularly as internal and external forces influence your content strategy, such as changes in the market, changes in the organization, and as new content is added to your strategy. Make plans to keep this document up-to-date to reflect any changes and keep it timely and relevant.

5. Chapter Bonus Material

Here are some additional best practices and bonus material specific to this chapter:

Atomizing Content

Content atomization is an extremely effective practice in content strategy and mainly applies to larger content pieces within the Awareness phase, such as eBooks, white papers, research surveys, and similar items. The way it works is by taking a large awareness asset, which is rich in content and substance, and converting its most salient elements into several individual and smaller content pieces. For instance, you may be able to take a large research survey recently completed by your company and then turn it into several individual blogs that discuss the findings (those blog pages can then link back to the web page where the gated survey lives).

You can also atomize your large content piece via social media by taking interesting facts or figures from a white paper and converting them into small bite-sized social media posts to be used on LinkedIn, Twitter, or Facebook. You can then link these posts back to your white paper. After writing, publishing, and promoting an eBook you can spin it off into presentations for thought-leadership webinars or industry-conference presentations. Whatever large content piece you create, think about how to atomize it so it can be as effective as possible. These large aware-ness content pieces are often referred to as *anchor content* because it anchors your content strategy by breaking up that large, rich content asset and turning it into several other smaller content assets that can be used many times, in different ways, and over a long period of time. **See Figure 6.**

Figure 6. Content Atomization

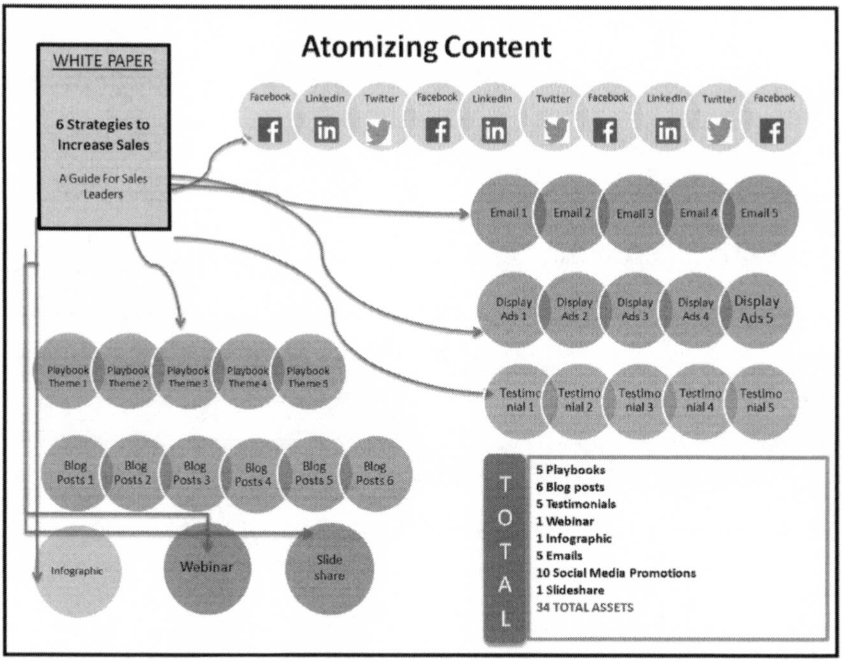

Conduct a Content Audit

A good practice before building out new content assets—especially if you are new to an organization or business unit—is to conduct a con-tent audit. A content audit is just as it sounds: it is the act of auditing any existing marketing content that has already been produced, and then categorizing it by content type and its phase in the buyer's journey. During the audit you may find that some content is old or irrelevant and needs to be retired and archived, while some may be new or still suitable for the market, and can potentially be repurposed.

Optimizing Content for Search

Optimize your content for search engines, specifically digital content assets such as landing pages, digital whitepapers, websites, and blogs. Working with your digital marketing and SEO teams in advance of building out content assets will help make certain your content is more easily found on search engines.

Using Calls-to-Action

Establish strong calls-to-action that promote other content, or that lead consumers of your content deeper down the buyer's journey. For example, you can have your blogs link to other content assets such as your website and white papers. You can have your white papers and case studies link to your website, other landing pages, or to your *contact us* page. With each content piece ask: *What do I want someone who consumes this content piece to do next?*

Don't Forget Other Audience Personas (Chapter 4)

Think about developing content that focuses on the end-user's story. This is a textbook example of *storytelling* marketing. Also, consider developing content assets that can be distributed, as appropriate, to your influencers. They can affect the decision-making process of your buyer, so it's best to think about how to get them on board with your offering or solution.

The Importance of Blogging

Blogs are consistently ranked the most trusted content on the Internet, so it should be a part of _every_ marketer's strategy. Blogs can offer an array of different content from thought-leadership visionary content to practical and instructional content. The calls-to-action on your blog site should not only encourage people to share those blog posts via their social and email channels, but also to subscribe to your blog forum or newsletters, this way they can be notified when new blog entries are published.

The Importance of Blog Copywriters for Executives

If your blog strategy includes using executives and existing clients as primary byline authors (which is recommended given the weight of their positions and thus weight of their message), then you should strongly favor having copywriters ghost-write on their behalf. Both your executives and clients are going to have busy schedules, so let them know that the blog can be ghost-written by someone else. Using their byline could drastically increase the amount of exposure the overall blog will receive out in the market than if it were bylined by someone who had less industry authority.

Insider Tips

To help you better build a content marketing framework here are a few resources I have found useful for me, personally, as a marketer, and that you may find useful too. The **Content Marketing Institute** can serve as an excellent external resource in helping you build up your overall content marketing knowledge. CMI is considered one of the leading content marketing organizations in the B2B marketing community. They specialize in advancing the practice of content marketing. Their training, certifications, blogs, articles, and thought-leaders can arm you with the knowledge you need to build a sophisticated content marketing strategy. Other content marketing resources include thought leaders such as **Michael Brenner**, CEO of Marketing Insider Group and author of *The Content Formula*; he, too, can be an excellent resource for you on the subject of B2B content marketing. Lastly, companies such as **Newscred** and **Kapost,** which specialize in enterprise content marketing platforms, can help you to manage, organize, publish, and promote content using their various web-based solutions.

CHAPTER 7

BALANCING THE
MEDIA MIX

Chapter Overview:

1. Overview of Media Mix Channels
2. Call-to-Action: Build a Media Mix Framework
3. Chapter Bonus Material

Balance the Media Mix is the last chapter in Section 2 focused on *Building*. Each chapter in this section was built on the one that came before it. Think about it for a minute—what you learned about building a *Buyer Persona Framework* (Chapter 4) contributed to the *Marketing Message Framework* (Chapter 5), which then contributed to the *Content Marketing Framework* (Chapter 6). Now all that's left to do is map that *Content Marketing Framework* to a balanced *Media Mix Framework*.

The media mix is comprised of four media channels: *Paid Media, Owned Media, Earned Media, and Social Media*. Creating a balanced media mix simply means that you are going to take all of the content you have developed and disseminate it via those four channels. The purpose of the balanced media mix is to broaden and diversify your reach to your target audience and maximize exposure of your content so that you increase the likelihood of more prospects consuming your information.

Look at it this way: if some of your buyers only seek out information via their social media channels, but your marketing strategy doesn't include the use of social media to deliver that information and content, then they will likely never learn about you, which could cost you. That's why it's a good idea to have a healthy and balanced media mix so you can increase the likelihood of exposing your content to more buyers.

In this chapter you will learn how to build a balanced media mix framework comprised of paid, owned, earned, and social media; and how to align it to your content marketing framework.

▶ 1. Overview of Media Mix Channels

Once you have developed your content assets, or have plans to develop them in the near future (think of the editorial calendar), you need to think through how to disseminate it to the market. So, how do you do that? How do you get people to read all this extraordinarily meaningful content you've created? The answer is that you have to take a multi-prong approach to getting it "out there." That means using multiple media channels.

See Figure 7. This figure illustrates how you can use paid, owned, earned, and social media as a vehicle to deliver your content to the market. Let's take a closer look at each of the four channels and at a few common examples of where these channels intersect.

Jason W. Simmons

Figure 7. Balanced Media Mix.

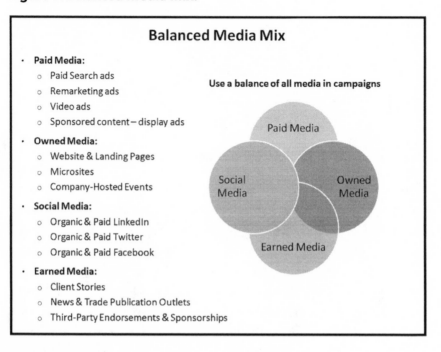

PAID MEDIA (Media activity which is purchased)

- Common Paid Media Examples:

    o Paid Search ads

        » Promote: White papers, eBooks, survey reports (other gated content)

    o Remarketing (display) ads

        » Promote: Contact us landing pages, gated content

    o Video ads

        » Promote: Powerful videos

    o Sponsored content distribution platforms

» Promote: Blogs and articles

Paid media allows you to promote your content simply by paying for it. This should be a part of any company's marketing strategy, but it's especially helpful for smaller companies that are less well-known in the market and that need to rely on a paid media strategy to get their message out in the market more prominently.

Because it costs to get your message out in the market through paid media, means that you need to get something valuable in return for your marketing dollars. For instance, gated content promoted through *paid search*, such as white papers, eBooks, or survey reports, requires someone to exchange their information in return for downloading and reading that high-valued content piece. Those who complete a form to retrieve that content will turn into top-of-funnel leads that can then be nurtured and turned into MQL's (marketing qualified leads), and thus potential pipeline revenue.

SEM (Search-Engine-Marketing) is commonly referred to as the strategy for managing any *paid search* engine activity (i.e. search engine ads and *remarketing ads* using search engines). When you think of paid media strategy, think SEM. This will be covered in a bit more detail, along with SEO (Search-Engine-Optimization), in the next chapter.

OWNED MEDIA (Media activity gained through assets a company or organization owns and controls)

- Common Owned Media Examples:

  o Website and Landing Pages that house:

    » Videos

    » Podcasts

    » White papers

- » Webinars

- » Case studies

- » Blogs

- » Infographics

- » Contact us form

- » Other content

- Microsites:

  - ○ Company-hosted events and forums

Owned media is just as it sounds: it is media you own, for example your website or landing pages that house your content such as blogs, podcasts, videos, and recorded webinars. It also includes microsites for the events and forums your company hosts.

One of the most important things to know about owned media is that your other media channels should be driving traffic to your owned media content (more on that in Chapter 8 Implement the Media Mix). For instance, if you are organically posting content on LinkedIn (social media), that post likely links to content that lives on a landing page you own, perhaps an infographic, podcast, or case study. Given that you're constantly driving traffic to your owned content, the goal, then, is to make sure your owned media content is user-friendly, engaging, and interactive for those who visit it.

EARNED MEDIA (Media activity generated by others through publicity or promotion)

- Common Earned Media Examples:

  - ○ Client Stories:

> » Client webinars

> » Client blogs

> » Client podcasts

> » Client case studies

> » Client video testimonials

> » Client presentations

o News & Trade Publication Outlets:

> » Press releases

> » News coverage

> » Guest blogs and op-eds

o Third-Party Endorsements & Sponsorships

> » External Industry Professionals or Thought-leaders

> » Professional partnerships

Earned media refers to instances where others promote your company, brand, or solution. This type of media can come from existing clients, endorsements from thought-leaders, or coverage from news media outlets, for instance.

Because earned media is the promotion of your brand/company by others, means it is very valuable and makes it an extremely effective way to build trust with your audience. It's one thing when you tout your own strengths—to an extent it is expected—but it is something completely different when others do it for you, especially when the praise comes from clients or objective third parties.

Reflect back on your buyer persona framework from Chapter 4 that details which media outlets or trade publications your buyers most commonly seek as their major source of industry news. Knowing that will help you prioritize which media outlets you should target to make your content visible.

SOCIAL MEDIA (Media activity gained on social media platforms)

- Common Social Media Examples:

    - LinkedIn

    - Twitter

    - Facebook

    - Instagram

    - Future platforms yet to be created

        » Promote: All content types

Social media should be used two ways: 1) as a vehicle to promote your content; and 2) as a way to engage and converse with followers and connections. (The next chapter will discuss more about how to use social media).

What makes social media unique is that most any content-type can be promoted using social media. No matter where the content falls within the buyer's journey, it can likely be promoted successfully via this channel. White papers, podcasts, case studies, videos, blogs, company-hosted events, and infographics should all be posted on social media.

PAID-SOCIAL MEDIA (Both paid media and social media)

- Common Paid-Social Examples:

    - Paid LinkedIn

- ○ Paid Twitter

- ○ Paid Facebook

- ○ Paid Instagram

- ○ Paid Future platforms yet to be created

  - » Promote: Gated Content

  - » Promote: Company hosted-events

Paid-social media simply means buying ad spots on social media platforms. Ads on social media sites easily blend in with organic posts, so there is typically high engagement in terms of clicks, views, and shares for social media ads versus other paid media ads. Because this is something you are paying for, you need to think strategically about what it is you want or need to promote.

In this case, gated content to generate top-of-funnel leads or a company-hosted event to generate registrations are excellent examples of how to use paid-social media. Also, paid-social allows you to target specific people or groups of people. For example, most paid-social ads, regardless of the platform allow you to target based on the groups people belong to, their geographic region, and the companies where they are employed.

OWNED-EARNED MEDIA (Both owned media and earned media)

- Common Owned/Earned Examples:

  - ○ Client content on your website

    - » Client blogs

    - » Client podcasts

    - » Client videos

» Client case studies

» Client webinars

Here's how you should view the difference between Earned Media and Owned-Earned Media: Earned Media is the act of your client telling their story, or the act of having an outside news article publish content that promotes your company, brand, or solution. Owned-Earned media is taking that story or article and giving it a place to live on your website or other owned media content so that you can drive traffic to it.

This can have a tremendous impact on those who then consume that content because it creates the opportunity for a prospect to get exposed to other powerful content. It also exposes the lead to your website where they can explore it further, learn more about your offering and brand, and engage in other calls-to-action.

PAID -EARNED MEDIA (Both paid media and earned media)

- Common Paid/Earned Examples:

  o Sponsored Content:

    » Sponsored research

    » Sponsored webinar

    » Sponsored article

    » Sponsored email

    » Industry conference sponsorship

    » Other sponsored media buys

Paid-Earned media primarily consists of sponsored content opportunities. These sponsored content opportunities include sponsored articles, sponsored webinars, and sponsored research. The content is sponsored by you but produced or published through a specific news outlet, trade publication, or professional trade association.

Paid-Earned opportunities are beneficial for a number of reasons, but primarily because they expose your brand to members of key organizations and to readers/members of those outlets. This helps to establish trust because your brand becomes associated with these news outlets and associations, which already have the trust of your buyers.

Sponsoring industry conferences is also an excellent way to promote your brand; these opportunities can result in receiving speaking sessions (presentations), and conducting focus groups with buyers.

Again, reference the Buyer Persona Framework that details which trade publications, professional trade associations, and industry news media outlets your buyers trust the most and commonly refer to for market and industry information. This will help to narrow your focus to the most appropriate outlets for media buys.

▶ 2. Call-to-Action: Build a Media Mix Framework

Now that you have a better idea about what makes up the media mix, the next step is to build the media mix framework. As mentioned in the beginning of this chapter, the goal of balancing the media mix is to maximize exposure of your content to the market; and the purpose of this framework is to map out how to do that using all four major media channels.

Exercise: Build a Media Mix Framework (don't forget to map it to your content strategy)

Before you begin this process, you should first refer to your Content Marketing Framework (from Chapter 6). That framework will list all of the marketing content that you currently own, or content that is planned for production in the future (as scheduled in the editorial calendar).

This media mix framework will take that content strategy and map it to the various media channels so you can have a plan for getting it out in the market. The framework will also create a balance within your media mix approach so you're not relying too heavily or too lightly on one particular channel.

Using the Marketing Strategy Working Document, create four columns, each corresponding to the 4 primary media channels: Paid Media, Owned Media, Earned Media, and Social Media. Under each Media category begin to list out all the tactics you just learned about or that you plan to use in your strategy. Here are some examples of what that might look like. **See Table 7.**

Table 7. Balanced Media Mix Framework

A Paid Media	B Owned Media	C Earned Media	D Social Media
Paid Search - Yahoo & Google & Bing:	**Website & Landing Pages that house:**	**Client Stories:**	**Organic - Facebook:**
Gated Content (anchor content)	White Papers (gated)	Client Webinars	All content types
Other important content	Blogs	Client blogs	Reply & Engage with Friends
	Recorded Webinars	Client Video testimonials	
	Case Studies	Client podcasts	
	Videos	Client Presentations	
	Podcasts		
	Infographics		
	Contact us Forms		
	Other		
Sponsored Content Distribution	**Microsite:**	**News & Trade Publication Outlets:**	**Organic - Twitter:**
Platforms to promote:	Company-Hosted Events or Forums Site	Press Releases	All content types
blogs		News coverage	Reply & Engage with Followers
podcasts		Guest blogs & Opeds	
other			
Remarketing Ads:	**Owned-Earned:**	**Paid -Earned:**	**Organic - LinkedIn:**
Gated content (anchor content)	Client content on website:	Sponsored Research	All content types
Company Website	blogs	Sponsored Webinar	Reply & Engage with Connections
Specific landing pages	case studies	Sponsored Article	
Contact us Forms	podcasts	Sponsored Email	
	videos	Sponsored industry conferences	
	and more	Other sponsored media buys	
Video Ads			**Paid - Social Media:**
Powerful videos ads on sites like Youtube			Company-hosted events
			Gated content

MEDIA MIX CHANNELS REMINDERS:
PAID & SOCIAL MEDIA ARE PRIMARILY USED TO PUSH TRAFFIC TO YOUR OWNED MEDIA CONTENT
PAID MEDIA: **MEDIA YOU BUY**
OWNED MEDIA: **MEDIA YOU OWN**
EARNED MEDIA: **OTHERS PROMOTING YOUR BRAND / CONTENT/ COMPANY**
SOCIAL MEDIA: **SOCIAL NETWORKING SITES**

Paid Media Column: List tactics such as *Paid Search*. Then, under the Paid Search heading, get more specific for what that paid search activity will consist of; for instance, to promote a gated white paper or research survey.

Owned Media Column: List assets such as *Website & Landing Pages*. Then, under the Website & Landing Pages heading get more specific for what that is; for example, these could be landing pages or web pages that house specific content such as your blogs, webinars, videos, gated content, white papers, and contact us submission forms.

Earned Media Column: List tactics such as *Client Stories*. Then, under the Client Stories heading get more specific for what client stories will consist of; for instance it may be client webinars, case studies, video testimonials, and client presentations (at conferences for example).

Social Media Column: List tactics such as *Organic LinkedIn*. Then, under the Organic LinkedIn heading, get more specific for what to promote via that social platform; for instance, this could be a good channel to organically promote press releases, podcasts, upcoming webinars, or a company-hosted event you are planning.

Continue to also build out your media mix strategy in the areas where two media channels intersect (i.e. Paid-Social, Owned-Earned, and Paid-Earned). By the time you have completed your framework you should feel confident that you have developed a thoughtful and deliberative strategy for getting your content out in the market via a number of media channels. You will now be ready to move into the next chapter *Implement the Media Mix*.

▶ 3. Chapter Bonus Material

Here are some additional best practices and bonus material specific to this chapter:

Calls-to-Action

In addition to having strong calls to action in your content, as was emphasized in Chapter 6, you should also have strong calls to action in your media mix. If you think about it, the entire media mix is really all about one thing: getting someone to do something, to take an action, such as to watch a video, read a blog, download a content asset, listen to a podcast, or register for an event. No matter if it's an organic social media post on Twitter, a paid ad on Google, or a social media ad on LinkedIn, you will always be driving someone somewhere. Given that, all of the media mix components should have strong calls-to-action. The more calls-to-action that your prospects engage in, the deeper your brand footprint and messaging will sink in with them.

Focus on Top-of-Funnel Leads

The media mix should be focused heavily on promoting top-of-funnel content to generate top-of-funnel leads. This is because, prospects, while they are in the education/awareness phase of the buyer's journey, are most interested in learning about the different solutions in the market that can help them solve their problem. They are essentially an open book and are eager to learn, therefore it is a prime opportunity to introduce them to your thought-leadership, perspective, and practical ideas on how you're able to help them solve those problems. The blogs, white papers, surveys, and other top-of-funnel content will be exactly what they are seeking. Once they are exposed to your top-of-funnel content, you can then gently guide them through the rest of their buyer journey exposing them to other content that's deeper down the funnel. Make sure your content and media mix tactics have strong calls-to-action that produce to top-of-funnel leads.

Inbound vs. Outbound Marketing (Pull vs. Push)

Most of this book's examples and recommended approaches to marketing tactics deal mainly with inbound marketing. For clarification, *inbound marketing* refers to marketing activity that **pulls** prospects into your content/message. For example, a paid search ad is clicked on by a prospective buyer who later turns into a marketing qualified lead for sales. In this example, the prospective buyer was searching for something online, found your ad that resonated, and then engaged with that ad; you pulled that prospective buyer in. *Outbound marketing*, on the other hand, is marketing activity that **pushes** your content/message to prospects. For instance, you deploy an outbound marketing email, it is then opened by a prospective buyer who engages in the *call-to-action*, and later turns into a marketing qualified lead for sales. In this example, the prospective buyer was not expecting your content or message, but engaged with the content and call-to-action anyway. When thinking through your media mix strategy place a heavier emphasis on the Inbound/Pull marketing rather than the Outbound/Push marketing. A marketing strategy that is centered on inbound marketing means a strategy that is going to drive higher quality leads, be much more three-dimensional, and is truly strategic.

Insider Tips

To help you better build a balanced media mix framework here are a few resources I have found useful for me, personally, as a marketer, and that you may find useful too. Organizations like **Hubspot** may help you think of some creative ways to develop a media mix strategy. This firm specializes in marketing automation software and other solutions, but they also regularly publish various content that can help you think through building a media mix strategy as well as a content strategy. They even offer various trainings and certifications on topics such as inbound marketing, which can greatly help you develop your media mix strategy muscles.

Web-based social media tools such as **Hootsuite** and **Sprinklr** can help you manage your social media strategy, these tools allow you to draft social media posts ahead of time and then deploy them later, at a date and time of your choosing. This, then, affords you the opportunity to put your social media on auto-pilot freeing up your time to do other important things. Lastly, a good thought-leader and marketer you should think about following on your social media channels is **Neil Patel**. Neil is a digital marketing expert and was named one of the top ten marketers by Forbes. He's always sharing and posting top-notch marketing content and can be an excellent resource for some of your own media mix strategies.

SECTION 3:
EXECUTE

Section 3 is centered on *Executing,* and includes Chapters 8-10. Here, you will take the content you developed from Chapter 6, and that was mapped to a balanced media mix framework in Chapter 7, and begin to effectively *execute* that media mix strategy. You will also enable the sales team for success by providing them with the tools and assets they need to be successful in their sales efforts. And, lastly, you will measure the performance of your marketing strategy once it's in-market, so you can ensure your goals and objectives are being met.

The first seven chapters of the book have been laser-focused on helping you build the blueprint for your marketing strategy. Chapter 8 will provide you the guidance on how to officially implement it. The remaining two chapters in this book, Chapters 9 and 10, will be centered on how to maintain success for your strategy once it's in-market.

Chapter 8: Execute the media mix by taking the balanced media mix framework, mapping it to a calendar, and executing on each of those individual components or tactics.

Chapter 9: Execute sales enablement activity by bringing in and delivering the tools and education needed to enable the sales team for sales success.

Chapters 10: Execute on a plan to measure your marketing strategy performance by establishing KPI's and benchmarks, and know how to optimize your strategy for improved success.

CHAPTER 8

IMPLEMENTING THE MEDIA MIX

Sun has what the world wants...

KEEP IT SAFE

 Sun microsystems

security.corp/keepitsafe/

completed the critical frameworks for your ~~message~~, content strategy, and media mix. You are now prepared to put the wheels in motion and implement your strategy!

In this chapter you will learn how to best implement each of the tactical components within each of the media channels so that your strategy performs optimally once in-market.

▶ 1. Overview on How to Implement the Media Mix

To help conceptualize the process of implementing a marketing strategy using all four media channels—paid, owned, earned, and social—I will repurpose the example from Chapter 1, *Trade Association Conference Success.*

Recall that in this example, your company sponsored an important industry conference and hired an industry thought-leader to serve as a speaker at a dinner you were hosting for prospects who were attending the conference. Using a thoughtful media mix strategy, take a look at the sponsored conference initiative with this new information in mind.

Example: Trade Association Conference Success – Revisited

In an effort to generate leads for sales and to create top-of-mind aware-ness in the market of your brand, you decided to sponsor a well-re-garded industry conference. This sponsorship is a prime example of **paid-earned media**. It's **paid media** because you paid for a spon-sorship, and it's **earned media** because the sponsorship agreement entailed that your brand logo be promoted and prominently displayed throughout the conference.

The thought-leader who attended and spoke at the dinner that you hosted during the conference is another example of **earned media.** The press release your company issued just prior to the conference and that informed the market of a big-named client you just signed, is yet again an example of **earned media**.

Leading up to the event, and in order to raise awareness with the market about your upcoming presence at the conference, you embarked on a social media campaign. That campaign included **paid-social media** ads on LinkedIn. Those ads targeted people who had specific job titles and who directly followed the trade association's social media account on LinkedIn.

Those paid-social ads directed traffic to a specific landing page on your company's website, which is an example of **owned media**. The landing page was created specifically to promote your company's presence at the conference, to increase RSVP's for the dinner, and to drive attendees to a breakout session being presented by a key client and a company executive during the conference. The client who was co-presenting with a representative from your company is another example of **earned media**.

Your colleagues who attended the conference readily shared their thoughts, photos, and takeaways of the event via tweets and posts on their social media accounts, helping to generate **organic social media** buzz.

As you can see, multiple media channels were implemented to make this important marketing initiative a success, though this example reflects merely one marketing initiative: a single sponsored event. However, your <u>entire</u> marketing strategy, when viewed over the course of several months to a year, will likely include many marketing initiatives; such as multiple conferences and webinars to manage, dozens of marketing content assets to promote, and a few big company-hosted events to lead. So, when implementing the media mix, ensure you are connecting each marketing initiative to the next – this will ensure your prospects are being guided seamlessly through the buyer journey and are being touched by many activities.

PAID MEDIA (Media activity which is purchased)

- Common Paid Media Examples:
    - Paid Search ads

» Promote: White papers, eBooks, surveys, reports (other gated content)

o Remarketing (display) ads

» Promote: Contact us landing pages, gated content

o Video ads

» Promote: Powerful videos

o Sponsored content distribution platforms

» Promote: Blogs and articles

Here are some common paid media examples that you may want to consider implementing into your media mix strategy to help drive traffic to your content / message.

Launch Paid Search Ads

Set up ad accounts with different search engine companies such as Yahoo, Google, and Bing, then bid on specific keywords that your buyers in the market are likely searching for on these search engines. When bidding on keywords, your ads will appear near the top or bottom of the search engine pages, thus getting potential prospects exposed to your content.

To help you determine which keywords to bid on, and to better manage your SEM strategy altogether, there are a number of SEM tools in the market that can help you identify which keywords are ripe for bidding and can help you manage your SEM strategy overall. As mentioned in the previous chapter, if your organization is not organically hovering near the top of search engine results pages (SERP's) for certain keywords, then this paid media tactic will help make up for that. Although it won't garner nearly the amount of clicks that come with a strong organic ranking, it nonetheless can help drive traffic to your content until you can build a better SEO strategy which is all about improving your organic ranking (SEO is discussed later in the chapter).

You don't need to be a pro at *paid search*, there is plenty of help out there to get you started. In some cases companies like Google dedicate custom SEM services through their internal marketing agencies to assist you with your SEM strategy. However these services may only be available depending on the amount of money you are spending with these search engine companies.

Set up Remarketing Ads

Remarketing ads should also be part of your SEM strategy. This works by tracking users who visit your website (tracked through Internet cookies). When prospects land on your website, your search engine analytics tools can track them and then target them with display ads as they continue to browse the web and visit other sites. Search engines are getting more and more sophisticated with remarketing ads that allow for more targeted remarketing; in these specific instances you are able to take a more precise approach to targeting only those who fit your buyer criteria.

For example search engines have a way of making assumptions about who you should serve remarketing ads to, based on other sites they have visited, and based on other information that was captured about them through data analytics. This deeper customer segmentation layered into the remarketing strategy means a higher ROI on remarketing spend.

Leverage Sponsored Content Distribution Platforms

Sponsored content is another excellent example of paid media and typically performs better than traditional ads. Sponsored content ads are simply ads that live on very specific websites, mainly news sites. They take on the appearance of a regular news article that is native to that site; however it is really just your ad with your content. People who are visiting these news sites are already looking for informational content, so your blogs or thought-leadership articles will likely perform well here.

OWNED MEDIA (Media activity gained through assets a company or organization owns and controls)

- Common Owned Media Examples:
  - Website & Landing Pages that house:
    - » Videos
    - » Podcasts
    - » White papers
    - » Webinars
    - » Case studies
    - » Blogs
    - » Infographics
    - » Contact us form
    - » Other content
  - Microsites:
    - » Company-hosted events & forums

Here are some common owned media examples that you may want to consider implementing into your media mix strategy, as well as ideas on how to get the most out of your owned media. The other media channels – paid, earned, and social should be used as a vehicle to drive traffic to your "owned media content".

Spruce up Your Website & Landing Pages

Think about how you can continuously make your owned media content enticing and relevant so that users who visit your website and landing pages are encouraged to stay longer, learn more, and take further actions.

For instance, turning PDF versions of white papers, surveys, or eBooks into digital and interactive media content, complete with interactive quizzes, video and audio snippets, visuals, images, and charts will transform your content into an active learning experience for users rather than a passive one. The goal is not to overwhelm them with content, but to use these interactive content components as a way to enhance their learning and understanding of the material.

Creating more digitized and interactive content on your website and other landing pages is more pertinent than ever before as people prefer to absorb content that is supplemented with media, images, pictures, video, audio, and quizzes. Web content that is too lengthy and text-heavy has become outdated.

In general, make it a best practice to upgrade and update your owned media so you keep up with how people prefer to navigate and consume web content. This will lead to improvements in your owned media performance, such as average *time on page*, *bounce rate*, and *total page views*. You also want to be sure to create visible calls-to-action throughout your owned media content so it is easy for people to know where and how to reach you when they are ready to engage one-on-one with a representative from your company.

Make Owned Content Shareable

To increase getting your message out in the market you need to make sure that your owned media content is *shareable*. Just like social media has "shareable" options built into it automatically (e.g. re-tweeting), so too should much of your owned media content be shareable. Design your landing pages and websites with options that grant readers the option to share it with others using social media, email, and other outlets.

Develop Microsites

Microsites can be built for specific activities or initiatives, such as when your company is hosting an in-person event (referenced in Chapter 6). In this example, these microsites will allow potential attendees of your event to view the agenda, speakers, conference theme, and other content as they contemplate attending.

Regularly Update Your Owned Media Content

Set up a periodic reminder, perhaps once a month or every other month, to make updates to the content that lives on your website. Perhaps you've just finalized some video content and now need to find a place for it to live on your site; or new features have been added to your solution offering and web copy needs to reflect those new features and benefits. Whatever it is, it's a good idea to get into a rhythm of updating the copy and content to your owned media assets.

EARNED MEDIA (Media activity generated by others through publicity or promotion)

- Common Earned Media Examples:
  - Client Stories:
    - » Client webinars

- » Client blogs

- » Client podcasts

- » Client case studies

- » Client video testimonials

- » Client presentations

  o News & Trade Publication Outlets:

  - » Press releases

  - » News coverage

  - » Guest blogs and op-eds

  o Third-Party Endorsements & Sponsorships

  - » External Industry Professionals / Thought-leaders

  - » Professional Partnerships

Here are some common earned media examples that you may want to consider implementing into your media mix strategy to help drive traffic to your content / message.

Capture Client Stories

Determine which of your clients have the most compelling or successful stories and find ways to capture those stories either through case studies, video testimonials, blogs, podcasts, or webinars. Earned media is the most powerful of all media, so being able to market client stories will go a long way in building credibility with other potential buyers who will likely relate to your existing clients.

Create an Advisory Board

One effective way to get client stories out in the market is by creating an advisory board. An advisory board, made up of existing clients, can benefit your organization and particularly your marketing organization in many ways. The board members can provide strategic advice to your organization; they can also dedicate their time and energy to promoting their story out in the market such as co-presenting a session at an industry conference, or agreeing to be interviewed for a podcast or a written case study. They can even offer to give input on marketing messaging, content, and more.

As new or successful client stories emerge within the advisory board, take note and find a way to promote it if and when possible. If you have the bandwidth and staff resources to dedicate to creating and managing an advisory board, then consider investing your time into that initiative as it will allow you to continuously promote a steady stream of compelling client stories in the market.

Write Guest Blogs & Op-Eds

By far, one of the most successful and effective marketing activities with respect to earned media is guest-blogging. This is where you secure opportunities with trade publications to write and be featured as a guest- blogger (a.k.a. op-ed contributor) on their site. The goal is to get your perspective out in the market on the specific news sites and trade publications that your buyers already trust and regularly read. In addition, getting your guest blog or op-ed article *back-linked* to your website will drastically improve your organic search rankings, and ultimately your SEO strategy, because it builds *authority* with your domain (see also the *Chapter Bonus Material* section).

To start this process, you need to work with your PR team who may already have relationships with these publications. Then, you will need to pitch a blog topic or abstract to the publication editor. If an editor believes that the blog content will be helpful, useful, or insightful to their readers, then there is a good chance they will agree to run your blog on their blog page. Editors at these trade publications need to continuously deliver fresh content to their readers, so they have some self-interest in working with you, too.

To increase the chances of getting a guest-blog published, you should make sure the blog content doesn't come across as too sales-y or too promotional. The editor needs his or her audience to receive valuable content that helps them solve a problem or think differently about a critical issue; try and avoid it sounding too "commercial." Also, if you are able to get an existing client to agree to byline the guest-blog, it will improve your chances of getting the article picked up. Your clients are likely in the same peer-group with the readership of these outlets, making it all the more credible from the Editor's perspective, and much more likely they will publish it.

Secure Endorsements: External Industry Professionals & Thought-Leaders

Securing endorsements from external industry professionals and thought-leaders is an effective method for establishing credibility of your company brand, or solution with the market. To get an idea as to how this might play out in a real life example, refer again to the Chapter 1 example *Trade Association Conference Success*. This is just one instance in which a thought-leader could help endorse your company, brand, or solution. They can also help by co-authoring white papers, securing meetings with key prospects, and participating in speaking engagements on your company's behalf.

Secure Endorsements: Professional Partnerships

In addition to seeking out thought-leaders for endorsements, you may also consider looking to other companies or organizations with which your company partners. For example, if your organization is partnering with companies such as Google, Amazon, or Microsoft, or perhaps smaller companies that are very well-known within your industry, this could make an excellent opportunity to receive endorsements for new products and solutions your company is launching, or an event your company is hosting. In addition to commercial partnerships, you can also consider building a partnership with professional trade associations within your industry. These trade associations (as have been discussed throughout the book) are already very credible with your buyers. Establishing some sort of paid or in-kind partnership or sponsorship with these associations will help to instantly create visibility of your company at their annual and regional conferences and other events throughout the year.

Issue Well-Timed Press Releases

Whenever there is an exciting announcement that needs to be made about your company or solution, publish a press release. Get creative with it in terms of when you issue press releases. For example, you can time your release to hit the market just prior to a big industry conference where you know your buyers will be attending. Once at the conference, your new press release will easily turn into conversation starters for your sales team who are attending that conference, and give your brand some heightened prominence going into the event.

SOCIAL MEDIA (Media activity gained on social media platforms)

- Common Social Media Examples:

    o LinkedIn

- o Twitter

- o Facebook

- o Instagram

- o Future platforms yet to be created

  - » Promote: All content types

Here are some common social media tips that you may want to consider implementing into your media mix strategy to help drive traffic to your content / message.

Consider Platform Types

Marketing content should be promoted differently based upon the social media platform you are using. For instance, on professional networking sites, such as LinkedIn, social media posts should come across professional and informative. That same content promoted on a non-professional networking site, such as Twitter can be less-formal, and even fun. As a general rule of thumb, it is a good idea to use images, gifs, or videos when posting on social media; these posts perform much better than those posts that only have text and no accompanying visual that entices a click.

Implement the Social 4-1-1 Rule

One big mistake many organizations make with their social media strategy is they make it all about them, so try to avoid situations where your social media posts are only about promoting *your* content. Social media is about having a dialogue, not a monologue, with the market. To do that you should follow the *social media 4-1-1 rule*. This rule states that for any given 6 social media posts you put out there, 4 should be re-sharing what others have posted e.g. re-tweets, shares, or reposts; 1 should be a response or reply to a post of a follower on your social channel; and 1 should be a post of *your* own content that you push out into the market. This is what it means to have a dialogue in the market through social media; it is when you are sharing other content from other users, replying and responding to followers, and initiating your own conversation with the market.

Implementing a 4-1-1 social media strategy or something similar (perhaps a 3-2-1 rule or 2-2-2 rule) will help you to avoid creating that monologue. The 4-1-1 strategy will not only increase your number of followers, but also increase the number of times YOUR content is getting shared by others in the market. This happens due to the reciprocity law that governs social media. That is when you share someone else's content, they are likely to reciprocate and share yours thereby increasing your chances of picking up new followers and getting additional brand exposure.

▶ 2. Call-To-Action: Implement the Media Mix

As you can see, there are a lot of moving parts when it comes to executing all these individual media mix tactics, and trying to manage it all at once can be challenging. That's why it's necessary to map out your media mix strategy to a calendar and have an organized plan for how to execute on it.

The goal of the media mix calendar is to do two things:

1) Map out your media mix strategy over a certain period of time. (In our example we'll assume a one year time frame to keep it consistent with the editorial calendar which is also scheduled over a one year time frame).

2) To track in real time all of the media mix components that are being executed.

Exercise: Create Media Mix Calendar & Implement Your Strategy

Using your Marketing Strategy Working Document begin to create the media mix calendar. **See Table 8a and Table 8b**. This is one table that has been broken into two sections (8a and 8b) so as to better fit within this book.

Table 8a. Media Mix Calendar (reflecting paid media & owned media)

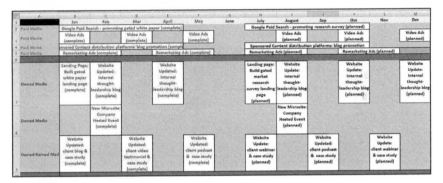

Table 8b. Media Mix Calendar (reflecting earned media and social media)

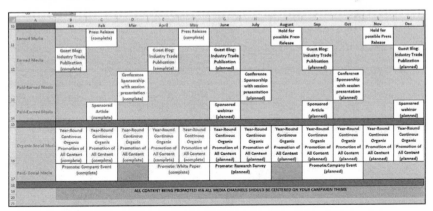

Start by creating a series of rows and columns; one column should list from top to bottom each individual media tactic that makes up your media mix strategy, and one row, moving from left to right should reflect each month of the year. You can then begin to layer in your media mix strategy by mapping each individual media tactic to the month of the year in which it will be executed. It's probably best to refer to your editorial calendar and Balanced Media Mix Framework, completed in Chapters 6 and 7, respectively, as you complete this exercise. This will help serve as a point of reference for you and will help you coordinate the timing of published content with the media mix calendar. For example, if you have plans to write a sponsored article (which is paid-earned media) in the month of September, you can simply slot it in you *paid-earned media* row and then under the *September* column. Here are some instructions to help you get started.

§ **Paid Media Rows** – For paid search ads or remarketing ads slot this under the appropriate months/columns during which those ads will be running. If you're running paid search for 4 months from January–April to promote various top-of-funnel content assets, then slot it under the January–April columns. Do the same for other paid media or paid-earned media opportunities. For instance, if you plan to sponsor three industry conferences during the year (paid-earned media) in the months of March, July, and October, you can slot each of those accordingly. Continue this exercise for all paid media tactics.

§ **Owned Media Rows** – As your website and landing pages get created or updated you will need to record it in your media mix calendar. For example, according to your editorial calendar you have several internal thought leadership blogs that are scheduled to be written and published on your company blog site in the months of February, April, August, October, and December. Slot that in your media mix calendar under each of those months/

columns. The same concept applies to owned-earned media content. If you have plans to produce a webinar featuring an existing client in the months of July and November, then slot it under those months/columns in your calendar once that content is living on your website. Continue this exercise for all other owned media tactics.

§ **Earned Media Rows** – Referencing your editorial calendar and Balanced Media Mix Framework, slot appropriate earned media content pieces into your media mix calendar. For instance, if you plan to secure guest-blog spots at certain points of time in the year, slot each of those under the appropriate months accordingly. Press releases can sometimes be hard to predict a year in advance, so place generic "Holds" in your media mix calendar for possible future press releases. However, once press releases are pushed out to the market in real time, then update this media mix calendar and slot it under the appropriate month in which that took place. Continue this exercise for all earned media tactics.

§ **Social Media Rows** – Social media is the vehicle that allows you to push almost any and all content. For your organic social media, plan to promote content year-round for all twelve months and have that reflected in your media mix calendar. Paid social, like your paid media, should be scheduled for however long you are running paid social ads. If you are running paid-social in January and February on LinkedIn to promote a company-hosted event, then slot that in your calendar appropriately.

Your media mix calendar, once complete, should display nearly every marketing tactic that will be a part of your marketing strategy and that you plan to execute over the next year. It should also be reflective of your media mix framework (from Chapter 7) and should align with the planned publishing of content as scheduled in your editorial calendar (from Chapter 6). This media mix calendar will serve as an organizing tool that provides direction for your marketing strategy in one simple and easy to understand visual.

Update your Media Mix Calendar in Real Time

As you progress through the year and execute on each of these individual pieces, you should make a note to mark each of them as complete. You can simply do this through color-coding, such as changing the font color on your document for each tactic from black to red or by simply labeling it "complete." For all the individual media tactics that have yet to be executed but that are planned out in the months ahead, you can list it in black font or simply label it "planned."

This document will be a living document that will require you to maintain and update it on a continuous basis. In a lot of ways this will serve as your month-to-month roadmap for *all* your marketing activity. It keeps you centered on your strategy, and keeps you focused on exactly what needs to be executed and when. You will need to reference it often and get into the habit of reviewing it and updating it on a regular basis as you progress through the year executing your strategy.

Expect Delays & Roadblocks in the Media Mix

Be prepared to deal with some delays and roadblocks from time to time that may keep you from executing on any one given media mix tactic. For example, a podcast you hoped to record that features a client has been postponed due to a last minute timing conflict with the client. This will require you to reschedule it on your editorial calendar and your media mix calendar until the client is available again. Another example is one in which you've run into some budget issues that will impact your paid media strategy, therefore resulting in a 1-2 month delay in starting Google search ads to promote your white paper. All in all, if you can execute on about 80% of your media mix strategy as planned within the timeline, then consider it a success.

3. Chapter Bonus Material

Here are some additional best practices and bonus material specific to this chapter:

SEO (Search Engine Optimization)

SEO is a marketing strategy that helps to improve the organic position or ranking of your website on a search engine's results page (SERP's). This is different than your SEM strategy, which is focused only on paid media via search engines. SEO requires a lot of work, as there are many organizations you compete with all clamoring to make it to the top of a SERP too, and all for the same or similar keywords. However, the more sophisticated your SEO strategy, the higher the organic ranking of your website relative to your competitors, and, thus, the more organic traffic you will drive to your website. Organic traffic produces higher quality and quantity visitors to your website than that which is produced through a paid media strategy (SEM is your paid media strategy).

There are three primary components that determine the organic ranking of a website on a SERP, and while there are many other factors that contribute to the ranking, these are weighted the heaviest within the SEO algorithm. These components include: 1) Authority; 2) Relevancy; and 3) Mobile-Optimization.

> *Authority is a numerical value that predicts how well a specific web page may rank on search engine results pages.*

To improve *Authority* means to improve the number of quality links that link back to your website or webpage. This "quality" refers to trusted sites, such as news sites, publication sites, and others that link to your webpages, from theirs. When search engine algorithms see that there is a healthy number of quality websites that link back to yours, the algorithm makes an assumption that you are clearly a leading authority in your field, and thus gives your page a higher score. The ways to improve your authority score include investing time and energy into writing guest-blogs and op-eds; there you will likely get an opportunity to back-link to your own website. Also, when your press releases are picked up by other news outlets (assuming you included the link to your website within that press release) it will result in a higher authority score. Lastly, sponsored articles (paid-earned media) are another way to get a quality and trusted website to link back to yours. All of these content pieces can be very effective at improving your authority score, and overall SEO strategy. If you can continuously find ways to secure guest-blogs, news articles, or sponsored-articles, then you will see your page authority continue to grow. Building authority should happen continuously, so plan to focus your SEO efforts here indefinitely.

> *Relevancy is the degree to which content on websites coincides with the keywords or search terms used. The more relevant your web content is to the search terms used, the greater the chance of receiving a more favorable position on SERP's.*

Relevancy is just as it might sound; it means your web content should be *relevant* to the keywords someone was searching. So, if your audience is searching for *data mining tools* then your website should be relevant to *data mining tools*. Something you should be careful of when it comes to "relevancy" is to not force certain keywords on your website because you think it might help you rank higher. The consequence may be a website or webpage that reads a bit awkwardly. Instead, think about what you want the user experience to be on your website. If your offering is relevant to *data mining tools* then you will likely be using the appropriate keywords, in your header titles and throughout the site, anyway. The good news is that search engines are smart enough to figure out if your website is relevant to what someone is searching, even if your web content doesn't have word for word matches with specific search terms. Search engine web crawlers find similar keywords on your site and makes assumptions based on those keywords. To ensure your website remains relevant, keep in mind the experience you want someone to have on your website, and chances are you will naturally build appropriate relevancy.

> ***Mobile-Optimization refers to websites that are adapted for mobile devices; websites which are not mobile-friendly result in poorer search rankings.***

Optimizing websites for mobile is a pretty standard practice now. People spend more time on the Internet through their mobile devices and tablets than on their laptop or desktop computers. Be sure your website is optimized for mobile devices such as smartphones and tablets.

Account-Based Marketing

Account-Based Marketing is a specific type of approach to B2B marketing, typically dealing with enterprise-wide sales deals, which target each individual account as if it were its own market. Overall, there are many different approaches to ABM. For instance, some marketing organizations may use 100% of their efforts to target only 4 or 5 prospect accounts, while others take a less-targeted approach (but an account-based marketing approach nonetheless) to target perhaps a few hundred accounts.

Account-Based Marketing is becoming more commonplace within B2B. As such, many marketing service and technology vendors are taking notice and developing solutions to help companies with their Account-Based Marketing initiatives. These solutions include tactics such as data-mining for compatible intelligence about specific accounts; targeting accounts with personalized display ads; and tracking website engagements of key accounts through marketing analytics tools. Should you partake in ABM activities, it's recommended you find the right marketing services and technology vendors to help you achieve your ABM goals.

Insider Tips

To help you better implement a balanced media mix here are a few resources I have found useful for me, personally, as a marketer, and that you may find useful too. First, it's important to call out that *Marketing Automation* is *the* cornerstone tool for any and all marketing activity, it is where campaigns are created, where they live, and where they flourish. It can't be emphasized enough that marketing automation is the lifeblood for marketing organizations, and without it, most marketing efforts are futile. There are several marketing automation platforms on the market, the most well known and prominent include **Eloqua by Oracle, Marketo, and Pardot**. Before B2B Marketing organizations invest in any software or web-based tool, they should first invest in automation.

Consider looking at organizations such as **MOZ and SEM Rush** to help you manage your SEO and SEM strategy. These organizations provide web-based tools that can help you in all facets of SEO & SEM, ranging from helping you with keyword research, increasing page and domain authority scores, and providing data & analytics insights.

Companies such as **Demandbase & Terminus** specialize in Account-Based Marketing and can help you target specific accounts by tracking your target accounts' IP address, and then hitting those accounts with personalized and direct display advertising. **Crazy Egg** is a tool that can help you manage and better understand your web traffic by providing you valuable data on site activity and engagement. For example it can report back specific data such as where on your page most people hover their cursor, how often people scroll, which CTA's people click, which they ignore or don't see, and more. Crazy Egg's heat maps and other solutions provide the valuable data you need to make the decisions how to best optimize your website. Overall, all of these tools listed here are evolving in sophistication all the time—which only helps you to better understand your marketing performance at a more granular level—so take advantage and use them often to enhance your strategy.

CHAPTER 9
ENABLING SALES

———

Chapter 9 Overview:

1. Assess Sales Enablement Needs
2. Enable with Education
3. Enable with Tools
4. Call-to-Action: Enable Sales
5. Chapter Bonus Material

Now that your strategy is in-market, the next step is to help enable the sales team for success. After all, the outcomes you are striving to achieve in your marketing strategy will be largely dependent on how successful the sales team is in their selling and prospecting efforts. This is why it is critical that they have the tools and training they need to succeed in their roles.

Historically, the sales enablement responsibility had largely been left to either the marketing team or sales team or both. However, this responsibility is beginning to rapidly evolve into its own stand-alone function, which means new sales enablement teams are emerging in order to be dedicated solely to this one task. The rise of sales enablement teams within organizations reflects the importance and prevalence this role has in improving sales efficiency, sales effectiveness, and organizational profitability.

Regardless if your organization has a sales enablement team or not, you will still likely contribute in some way to the sales enablement process, either by working with the sales enablement team as a conduit into the sales team, or by working with the sales teams directly. Because each organization may have some nuances with respect to where the sales enablement responsibility falls, this chapter will present some standard baseline sales enablement guidelines, steps, and examples you can refer to and apply as needed, depending on the level of ownership you have for this responsibility.

In this chapter you will learn how to assess the sales enablement needs of the sales team and how to provide them with the tools and training they need to be successful in their sales efforts.

▶ 1. Assess Sales Enablement Needs

It's recommended you meet with your sales leader and a few individual sales reps to assess their sales enablement needs; meeting with several members on the sales team is important as it allows you to tap into a wide ranging and diverse pool of thought about how they view their challenges and the potential solutions to help them address those challenges. Also, consider meeting with a few individual reps who have varied levels of sales success and tenure in the organization—this is to better ascertain the broad spectrum of sales enablement needs that exist among the team.

Though you will need to meet and engage with different members of the sales team to learn about where they most need help to perform better in their roles, you will also need to acknowledge that sometimes the sales team simply doesn't know what they need. Asking what tools or training would be helpful for them may not yield the desired results you had hoped for. Therefore, the best way to approach these conversations is to work backward to attempt to find out what their challenges and needs are, and then create a solution from there.

Instead of asking questions such, as "What do you need to be successful?", ask questions that may be specific to potential struggles, such as where they have difficulty in prospecting or closing, where redundancies or time-wasters exist within the sales process, how confident they are in speaking to prospects about the market, their knowledge on solution and product features, or competitors. This may help you more easily find solutions that will help solve the challenges you uncover.

2. Enable with Education

A famous quote comes from 19th century English philosopher Herbert Spencer: "The great aim of education is not knowledge but action." In a lot of ways, educating or training sales people is really about empowering them to *act* more effectively, efficiently, and confidently—all of which is needed to yield positive outcomes.

There are a plethora of subjects and topics to choose from when thinking about sales enablement training. For instance, all of the research you spearheaded around competitors, market analysis research, and buyer persona research, as recommended in earlier parts of the book, is a good place to start. Not only does this research help you as a marketer to build a marketing strategy, but sharing it with sales members can help them be more effective in their sales strategy, too. As was also mentioned earlier in the book, it is a good rule of thumb to continue conducting these types of research on a continuing basis because markets, buyers, and competitors change all the time, and being able to adapt to those changes is critical.

Below are a few common training topics that could be of value to the sales team. The information they gain from these trainings will help them be more effective when talking to prospects and when trying to move a deal through the pipeline.

Training on Buyer Persona Research

As you conduct and complete buyer persona research, consider providing an overview of your findings. The buyer persona research will give sales the insights they need about where buyers are expressing discomfort and challenges, what solutions they are shopping in the market, and why they are looking at specific solutions. This training will help sales better speak the buyer's language, know them more intimately, and connect with them personally.

Training on Competitors

As you conduct and complete competitive analyses consider providing an overview of your findings. The findings of your competitors may include a wide array of insights such as their business model, value proposition, web presence, campaign theme(s), marketing strategy, media share-of-voice, market share, and market presence. This information will help sales know how they can better position their own message in a way that maximizes differentiation and stresses the value proposition. Having a better understanding of competitors will afford sales reps the opportunity to more confidently explain why their offering, solution, or brand is different and better.

Training on Win-Loss Analysis

As sales reps experience both successes and failures with deals in their pipeline, attempt to conduct win/loss analyses trainings. Find out what went right on a deal that turned it into a *closed-won*; and what went wrong on a deal that turned it into a *closed-lost*. Then, partner up with the rep who worked on these deals and share those findings in detail with the larger sales group. Of all the sales-enablement training to be conducted, this can be the most valuable. This training will help sales know which pitfalls to avoid when moving a deal through the pipeline, and which winning strategies help contribute to closed-won deals.

Overview of the Marketing Strategy

As you put the final touches on your strategy and are just beginning to execute on it (Chapter 8) present a high-level overview of your strategy to the sales team. It's crucial for them to get a well-rounded view of what you have created and how it impacts them. The purpose of sharing this information with sales is to inspire their confidence in the marketing strategy, and to offer them a view into what future marketing activity is happening, and how they will likely benefit. For example, knowing when they might expect new leads or knowing how certain activity/events might help to accelerate their prospects in the pipeline.

 ## 3. Enable with Tools

To help enable sales people for success in all phases of the selling process—identifying, prospecting, engaging, and converting—means you will need to enable them with specific content tools and technology tools to help them realize that success. It goes without saying that there are many sales enablement technology tools on the market, and as technology advances, so, too, does sales-enablement technology advance. The tools listed here are examples that will likely evolve in the years to come while new tools emerge.

TECHNOLOGY SPECIFIC TOOLS

Sales Enablement Systems

There are many different sales enablement platforms in the market and all offer a number of solutions. These include solutions such as **content management tools, analytics and reporting,** and **digital playbooks**, and most all integrate with CRM Systems such as Salesforce. Here is a brief overview of some of the more common and widely-used solutions within these platforms, and just some of the features that are offered.

Content management tools are web-based or software solutions that house, and make accessible, marketing collateral to sales. This tool helps sales teams more efficiently find, browse, and access marketing collateral that they can then use when talking to prospects (rather than digging around on their desktop or shared folder looking for content assets).

When integrated with a CRM system, sales reps will receive automated suggestions about how and when to use specific content assets based on a particular lead record or sales opportunity record stage within the CRM system. For example, if your sales rep, Jennifer is working a lead that she just received and that is in **new status**, the system may provide her a recommended white paper, blog, recorded podcast, or webinar that may be most pertinent to send to that new lead. Similarly, if Jennifer is working a lead that is in **working status** and farther down the pipeline, the system may recommend different content assets, such as a customized demo or a particular case study. This is all about improving sales efficiency and effectiveness.

Analytics and reporting tools help to capture analytics around how often a particular marketing asset is being accessed and used by sales, and where it is being used within the buyer's journey. These details and data points will help marketing team members easily identify high-performing content, low-performing content, and help them adjust their content marketing strategy accordingly.

Custom digital playbooks are really digital training assets for sales and can be used to quickly train sales reps on specific products or solutions with which they may not be familiar. For instance, these digital playbooks provide a short summary of a particular product or solution, the buyer persona, value proposition, pricing, and competitors. This summary is delivered via short videos, audio recordings, client quotes, snippet descriptions, high-level overviews, or optional access to full-length marketing content. Its purpose is to very quickly make it easy for a sales rep to breakdown and understand a complex or complicated solution in a matter of a few brief minutes.

CRM & Marketing Automation Integration

Integrating a CRM system with Marketing Automation can deliver real value for sales. The CRM system is likely being used by the sales team as a way to manage leads and sales opportunities in the pipeline; and the marketing automation system is likely being used by the marketing team to capture, nurture, and score leads as they engage in marketing activity.

Integrate these systems so that when a lead is captured, created, and scored in a marketing automation system (through marketing activity), it is simultaneously created in the CRM system as a new lead record and transferred to sales for further qualification and follow up. The integration as described will allow for lead records within a sales CRM system to reflect the marketing activity that was captured through the marketing automation system.

For example, Mark, a prospective buyer, visits your website, downloads some gated content assets, and listens to a podcast—all within a two week period. The marketing automation system captured and logged all of Mark's activity and assigned it a lead score; it then automatically created a lead record for Mark in CRM and routed it to your sales reps' lead queue for follow up. All of Mark's engagement during the past two weeks is fully visible to your sales rep. These types of deep insights about Mark's engagement history will put the sales rep in a stronger and more knowledgeable position before he initiates a conversation with Mark.

Account-Based Intelligence Tools

By using sophisticated search engine crawling and data-mining, ABI tools are able to report back key information about key target accounts your sales team is actively pursuing and that would be of direct relevance to sales reps. ABI tools accurately capture which accounts, and contacts within those accounts, are associated with news articles, blogs, posts, or press releases that directly match the keywords, subjects, and topics that would be of interest to sales reps. For instance, an ABI tool may pick up that a buyer at your key target account was recently quoted in an industry news outlet referencing subject matter that directly relates to your marketplace.

This information would make it extremely valuable to a sales rep who then may want to quickly engage that prospective buyer and reference their quote in that news article, thereby creating customized and personalized outreach. These ABI tools also feature sophisticated email templates that in a few clicks will automatically draft and send that personalized email which references that relevant content on behalf of the sales rep. This drastically improves efficiency in the prospecting process.

This type of tool provides all of the information a sales rep would need about a key contact at an account, such as their contact information, social media profiles, and relevant online articles, documents, or content that is specific to that contact.

CONTENT SPECIFIC TOOLS:

Best-in-Class Presentations

When sales is presenting to prospective buyers, not only does the message need to resonate in a deep and meaningful way, but also the design and creative elements of that presentation needs to resonate in a deep and meaningful way. Finding a good PowerPoint or Prezi designer to help you build and maintain your sales and pitch decks will be a worthy investment.

Cut-and-Paste Email Templates

Cut and paste templates are really about saving the sales team time more than anything else. These email templates can be created for a variety of purposes, such as inviting prospects to a company-hosted event, introductory emails for inbound leads, outreach to prospects who are attending an industry conference to set up meetings, and more.

4. Call-to-Action: Enable Sales

There is a lot that can be done—and that should be done—to enable the sales team for success. It's recommended you create and maintain a log of all the sales enablement tools, education, and engagements that are taking place or that are being provided to sales. The purpose of this log is to help you organize the sales enablement activity and keep a running record of it.

Exercise: Create the Sales-Enablement Log

Using your Marketing Strategy Working Document create three columns and label each column as *Roll-out Date*, *Sales Enablement Activity*, and *Sales Enablement Activity Type*. **See Table 9.** As you go through the process of enabling the sales team, either by providing training, technology tools, or content tools, you should record that activity using this log.

Table 9. Sales Enablement Log

	Roll-out Date	Sales Enablement Activity	Sales Enablement Activity Type
1	Roll-out Date	Sales Enablement Activity	Sales Enablement Activity Type
2	03-2016	Buyer Persona Research	Education / Training
3	05-2016	Market Analysis Research Training	Education / Training
4	08-2016	Inbound MQL Follow up Email Template	Tools / Assets
5	09-2016	Industry Conference outreach Email Template	Tools / Assets
6	10-2016	Marketing Automation & CRM Integration - Roll out	Tools / Assets
7	11-2016	New Sales Pitch Deck Created	Tools / Assets
8	01-2017	Brand Analysis Overview	Education / Training
9	02-2017	New Sales Enablement Content Tool - Roll out	Tools / Assets
10	03-2017	Account Based Intelligence & Prospecting Technology Tool - Roll ou	Tools / Assets
11	04-2017	Competitor Analysis	Education / Training
12	04-2017	Sales Enablement Content Tool & CRM Integration - Roll out	Tools / Assets
13	07-2017	Sales Enablement Tool - Refresher Training	Tools / Assets
14	08-2017	Prospecting Email Template	Tools / Assets
15	09-2017	Content Pack	Tools / Assets
16			

I'll use a couple of examples as context for how you can do this. Let's say you've recently conducted a focus group with buyers in your market for the purpose of updating your buyer persona framework. You've also recently shared those intricate details and findings with the sales team via a training and overview. To record that activity in your sales enablement log, simply list the date you completed that training with the sales team in the *Roll-out Date* column; list the activity you completed, in this case it was *Buyer Persona Research* in the *Sales Enablement Activity* column; then list the sales enablement type, in this case *Education & Training*, in the *Sales Enablement Activity Type* column.

Here's another example: you recently integrated your company's CRM system and Marketing Automation system, and then rolled out the new features to the sales team. To update the sales enablement log, list the date these features were rolled out to sales in the *Roll-out-Date* column; then list the activity, in this case *Marketing Automation & CRM Integration* in the *Sales Enablement Activity* column; and then list the activity type, in this case *Tools / Assets* in the *Sales Enablement Activity-Type* column.

5. Chapter Bonus Material

Here are some additional best practices and bonus material specific to this chapter:

Insider Tips

To help you better enable the sales team here are a few resources I have found useful for me, personally, as a marketer, and that you may find useful too. Sales enablement platforms such as **SAVO** offer solutions for content management, analytics and reporting, and custom digital playbooks that power sales reps for success by providing them the sales content, coaching, and enablement assets needed to make their prospecting engagements more effective and efficient. *Customer Relationship Management* (CRM) systems such as **Salesforce** can help sales teams manage their day-to-day engagements with leads, contacts, and opportunities in the pipeline, and it can also integrate with other systems such as *marketing automation systems* and sales enablement platforms. **Demandbase** offers a range of *Account-Based Marketing* solutions, one of which is an account-based-intelligence tool that offers keen insights about target accounts and target buyers. Lastly, **Sharpslide**, a small firm that specializes in creating cutting-edge presentations, can be an excellent resource for building best-in-class sales decks and other presentation content for important meetings.

CHAPTER 10

MEASURING MARKETING PERFORMANCE

Chapter 10 Overview:

1. How to Measure
2. What to Measure
3. Call-to-Action: Build a Quarterly Performance Dashboard
4. Chapter Bonus Material

Your marketing strategy is now being executed via a balanced media mix, your sales team has the tools and assets they need to be successful in their sales efforts, and all that's left to do is monitor and measure the performance of your strategy to certify it is on track for success. To measure the performance of your strategy means you need to look at each individual component of that strategy and assess whether it is helping to deliver on your goals and objectives.

In this chapter you will learn how to measure success for your marketing strategy, what it is you need to measure, and how you can go about making adjustments to your strategy to improve and optimize its performance.

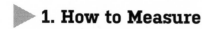 # 1. How to Measure

By now you should have identified and implemented into your marketing plans the goals and objectives for your marketing strategy. If you remember, the goals and objectives of your strategy were covered in the *Introduction*. Now is the time to learn how you can measure those goals and objectives by using Benchmarks and Key Performance Indicators (KPI's). Goals, Objectives, Benchmarks, and KPI's all work together when measuring the performance of your strategy. Here is a quick definition for each, and an example of how they interconnect.

Goal: A goal is a desired outcome you set out to achieve.

Objective: An objective is the desired-action needed to achieve that desired outcome.

Benchmark: A benchmark is a reference, value, or metric against which KPI's can be compared or measured.

Key Performance Indicator (KPI): A *key performance indicator* is a quantifiable measurement of a particular activity that helps determine success when achieving a particular objective.

That may sound like a lot to absorb, so to more easily grasp these definitions here is an example for how these elements would be used in a B2B Marketing scenario – and specifically how they relate to one another. Let's say your **goal** at the beginning of a calendar year is to source 10% of sales pipeline revenue for that year through marketing activity. To help you achieve that goal, you determine that your **objective** is to produce 100 marketing qualified leads by the end the year for the sales team. As a **benchmark**, you aim to produce 25 MQL's each quarter of the year. The number of leads you *actually* produce each quarter is a **key performance indicator** and indicates how likely you are to achieve your objective.

This is how it breaks down per this scenario:

Goal = Source 10% of sales pipeline revenue through marketing activity for the year

Objective = Produce 100 marketing qualified leads for the sales team by end of year

Benchmark = Generate 25 MQL's per quarter (this is the goal to measure the KPI)

KPI = the actual number of MQL's generated each quarter

In addition to measuring outcomes, as in the above example, B2B Marketers must also measure costs. For example, if a $50k lead-gen activity produces 25 high-quality leads (BANT criteria met) resulting in a $2k CPL, and a different lead-gen activity that costs $40k also produces 25 leads of equal quality (BANT criteria met) resulting in a $1.6K CPL, then those cost outcomes should be factored into your future lead-gen plans so that you maximize your marketing budget and improve ROI. This is a cost-based KPI. Other factors outside of CPL should also be factored into your calculation when determining which lead-gen activities to pursue. For instance, a lead sourced from an industry conference may cost more than leads sourced from other activities, however that conference lead may have a higher conversion rate once in the sales funnel, resulting in a greater likelihood of turning into pipeline revenue.

▶ 2. What to Measure

Because everyone reading this may have different marketing strategy goals and objectives, and thus will need different KPI's to measure those different goals and objectives, it is perhaps best to cover some of the most common B2B marketing KPI's and metrics that are found in most B2B marketing strategies. You can then apply the appropriate KPI's and metrics to your own marketing strategy. It should be prefaced that this is not a complete and entire list of every marketing KPI or metric, but rather a list of those that are most common. Some of these KPI's and metrics may be pertinent to you, others may not, and some may not be on this list at all—use, discard, or add from this list as needed.

To make it easier to manage and organize the long running list of potential KPI's and metrics you may use to measure your marketing strategy's goals and objectives, it may make more sense for you to categorize or bucket these KPIs and metrics into four specific groups. These groups will be labeled *Who Saw, Who Engaged, Who Converted* and *Who Became*.

WHO SAW

This should deal with any KPI's or metrics around those who have seen, viewed, or been exposed to your content, message, or story.

KPI / METRIC	WHAT IT IS	HOW TO IMPROVE (if applicable)
Total Page Views	The total number of views a particular webpage has received.	Increase the number of sources, channels, and activities you have that drive traffic to your site.
Bounce Rate	The percentage of visitors to a page or site who then leave or navigate away from the site. It is a single page session on your site.	Ensure your website content is relevant to what people were searching so that it meets their content expectations, and so they navigate the site.
Time on Page	The amount of time a visitor spends visiting a particular page on your site before leaving.	Make sure web content is useful, pertinent, and informative so it encourages people to read and stay longer.

Pages-per-Session (average)	The average number of pages viewed on your site, within one site visit/ session.	Make sure navigation features and calls-to-action are prominently displayed so it's easier for people to navigate your site and so that they are encouraged to explore further. Give people a reason to check out and view other pages. Web content must meet the content expectations of people who visit your site.
Impressions	A single display of your ad on a webpage.	
Email Open Rates	The percentage of people on an email list (within an email campaign), who open a particular email.	Be sure to target the right audience and titles with the right message. Ensure that the subject line is appropriate, thought-provoking, or action-oriented.
Cost-per-Impression (CPM)	The cost per 1,000 advertisement impressions on a particular web page.	Improve CPM by improving the number of clicks you receive. This can be done by placing ads above the fold on a website, making them more easily found, and ensuring the ads are germane to the site on which they appear.
Media Share-of-Voice	Media share-of-voice is the percentage of all web content mentions your brand or company receives relative to your competitors. If your brand was mentioned 100 times in the media and the total number of mentions among you and all your competitors was 500, your media share-of-voice would be 20%. * 100/500 = 20%	Work with public relations team to produce more content that is likely to be covered or picked up by outside news outlets. Participate in more guest-blogging opportunities and op-eds.

SEO (See Chapter 7)	Search Engine Optimization	To improve organic ranking of your website on search engines, make improvements to your site as it relates to authority, relevancy, and mobile-usability.

WHO ENGAGED

This should address any KPI's or metrics around those who have interacted, engaged with, or experienced your content, message, or story.

KPI / METRIC	WHAT IT IS	HOW TO IMPROVE (if applicable)
Total Clicks (ads)	The total number of clicks an ad receives.	
Click-Through-Rates (CTR's)	The total number of clicks an ad receives divided by the total number of times that particular ad is shown (impression). A total of 20 clicks for an ad that had 1,000 impressions would equal 2% CTR. * 20 / 1,000 = 2%.	See how to improve Cost-per-Impression (CPM).
Conversions	When someone clicks into your ad and then completes the call-to-action, such as download gated content or click into another page.	

Conversion Rates	The number of conversions divided by the total number of ad clicks (actions taken). For example, if your ad had 1,000 clicks and 35 conversions came from those clicks the conversion rate would be 3.5%. * 35/1,000 = 3.5%.	To improve conversion rates on search engines add under-performing keywords to your negative keywords list - if certain keywords are not generating the engagements you desire, adding them to your negative keyword list will keep them from appearing when those keywords are searched—saving you money and increasing conversions. Also, make sure your overall keyword list is targeted, accurate, and specific.
Cost-per-Click (CPC)	The total cost or price paid for an advertisement divided by the number of clicks that ad receives. For instance, an ad that costs $1,000 and received 320 clicks would equal $3.12 CPC. * 1,000/320 = $3.12	Make sure that your ad is being displayed to the appropriate audience by making sure you bid on appropriate and correct keywords on search engines, your remarketing efforts are targeted, and your display ads appear on appropriate websites your prospects are likely to visit. Also, your ads need to be strategically placed, to increase its visibility.

Cost-per-Action (CPA)	The total cost spent on an ad divided by the total number of desired actions that came from that ad (for clarification, desired action would be the action that person took after clicking into that ad, and something that you had hoped for, such as downloading gated content. This is the difference between *cost-per-click* and cost-per-action). For example, an ad that costs $1,000 and received 16 desired actions would mean the cost-per-action is $62.50. *$1,000/16 = $62.50.	
Event & Webinar Attendees	The total number of attendees who attend an event, webinar or some other direct or virtual engagement.	There are a number of ways to increase turnout or registrations at such events, such as widening the target list, heavier promotion, and broadening the topic to attract a more diverse audience. The focus here should be on improving both quality and quantity attendees.
Social Media Shares & Engagements	The total number of engagements or actions taken on a social media post, such as liking, sharing, or retweeting.	Using images, videos, or other media can help attract people to your social media post. Also, the more valuable the content the greater the likelihood it will be shared.

Email Click-Through-Rates	The total number of unique clicks inside an email divided by the total number of email addresses that received that email. A total of 40 clicks in an email that had 1,000 email recipients would equal 4% email CTR. * 40/1,000 = 4%.	Have strong, visible calls-to-action; reference the same link multiple times; include video, images, or other media content that entices someone to click.
Content Downloads	The total number of people who download marketing content; typically gated content.	Ensure it is a high-value content piece and that the message is relevant, thought-provoking or helpful.
Contact Us Form Submissions	The total number of people who complete a *contact us* form submission requesting to speak with a company representative. Also referred to as a "hand-raiser."	Ensure nurture emails, and other owned, earned, paid, social media has visible and strong calls-to-action that lead prospects to contact us forms—especially when they are nearing the end of their buyer's journey.

WHO CONVERTED

This should deal with any KPI's or metrics around those who have converted into marketing qualified leads and pipeline opportunities.

KPI / METRIC	WHAT IT IS	HOW TO IMPROVE (if applicable)
Total Number of MQL's Generated	The total number of marketing qualified leads generated. It is the aggregate of all leads generated from all lead sources that stem from all lead-gen initiatives.	

Average Cost-per-Lead (CPL) (See Chapter 3)	The cost paid on average to produce one marketing qualified lead. It is calculated by taking the marketing budget devoted to all lead-gen initiatives or campaigns and dividing it by the total number of leads actually generated. *$100k budget / 50 MQL's generated = $2k Average CPL.	Assess the outcomes of all lead-gen campaigns or initiatives to determine which produce the highest ROI by producing the lowest cost-per-lead. You also need to factor in conversion rates in the sales funnel by lead source.
Marketing-Sourced Sales Opportunities (See Chapter 3)	Sales opportunities in the pipeline that came from leads that were produced directly from marketing activity (i.e. lead came from content campaign and was nurtured and passed to sales).	
Marketing-Influenced Sales Opportunities (See Chapter 3)	Sales opportunities in the pipeline that were influenced by marketing activity somewhere along the buyer journey, but only after the lead had already been generated by sales (i.e. lead was acquired by sales through cold-call but later engaged in some sort of marketing activity such as attended webinar or downloaded marketing content).	

WHO BECAME

This should deal with any KPI's or metrics around those leads that turned into paying clients and won-deals.

KPI / METRIC	WHAT IT IS
Average Customer Acquisition Cost (See Chapter 3)	The total marketing cost paid on average to produce one paying client or won deal. * $200k budget / 10 clients acquired = $20k ACAC.
Customer Lifetime Value (see Chapter 3)	The calculated prediction of revenue gained from the future relationship with a client. Formula: Average annual revenue contributed by client, multiplied by average number of years a client remains a client, subtracted by the average customer acquisition cost. * $150k average annual revenue x 5 years average - $20k ACAC = **$730k CLV.**
Marketing-Sourced Closed-Won Revenue (see Chapter 3)	Marketing-sourced sales opportunities that turn into closed-won deals and clients.
Marketing-Influenced Closed-Won Revenue (see Chapter 3)	Marketing-influenced sales opportunities that turn into closed-won deals and clients.
Net Promoter Score	A measurement that is used to gauge customer loyalty by assessing how likely a client is to recommend your company or solution to others. NPS score is on a range of 0-100.

Using the four categories *Who Saw, Who Engaged, Who Converted* and *Who Became,* you should have a better idea about how you can assess the performance of your marketing strategy. As a reminder, there may be different KPI's and metrics you will want to use based on your strategy's goals and objectives. For instance, if one of your goals is to improve brand favorability within the market, then an objective may be to implement a sophisticated personalized ad campaign highlighting your brand.

Your KPI's can then be centered on metrics around: time on page, click-through-rates, total conversions, and cost-per-conversion. These KPI's will tell you more about how well your ads are performing in order to increase brand favorability. It's important to look at the *Who Saw, Who Engaged, Who Converted,* and *Who Became* KPI's and metrics through the prism of your specific marketing strategy's goals and objectives and measure your strategy accordingly.

▶ 3. Call-to-Action: Build a Quarterly Performance Dashboard

In an effort to help you manage your marketing strategy's specific KPI's and metrics, you should track and review those KPI's and metrics on a quarterly basis. Tracking all of these components regularly will help keep you centered on exactly what it is you are trying to achieve and how your strategy is performing as it relates to your benchmarks. After all, it is very easy to get lost in the day to day grind of executing your strategy, and every once in a while you just need to take a step back and assess its performance.

Exercise: Build a Quarterly Performance Dashboard

Here's how you can track and review your strategy's performance. Using your Marketing Strategy Working Document create a Quarterly Performance Dashboard; the purpose of this dashboard is to monitor and measure, on a quarterly basis, all of the relevant KPI's and metrics that are helping you to deliver on your marketing strategy's objectives.

To get started, create four columns and label them each *Who Saw, Who Engaged, Who Converted,* and *Who Became* KPI under each column, list your strategy's specific KPI's and metrics that correspond accordingly to that category. For example:

WHO SAW: List KPI's and metrics around Page Views, Time on Page, Impressions, Pages-per-Session, etc.

WHO ENGAGED: List the KPI's and metrics around Total Clicks, Event/Webinar Attendees, Content downloads, Social Media shares/engagements, Total Conversions, Cost-per-Action, etc.

WHO CONVERTED: List the KPI's and metrics around MQL's generated, Average CPL, Pipeline Opportunity that has been sourced or influenced through marketing efforts

WHO BECAME: List the KPI's and metrics around Customer Acquisition Cost, Customer Lifetime Value, Closed-won deals that were sourced or influenced through marketing efforts

See Table 10. This table will demonstrate how your dashboard should look once completed.

Table 10. Quarterly Performance Dashboard.

A	B	C	D
QUARTERLY PERFORMANCE DASHBOARD: CURRENT QUARTER: Q2			
WHO SAW? Impressions, Page Views, Share of Voice	WHO ENGAGED? Acted, Attended, Downloaded, Contacted	WHO CONVERTED? Conversion Metric: Leads & Opportunities	WHO BECAME? Became Clients
Time on Page: 3:05	Total Clicks: 8.2K	MQL's Generated Total: 24	Average Customer Acquisition Cost (ACAC): $33K
Email Open Rates: 22%	Click-Through-Rates: 1.8%	Average CPL (Cost-Per-Lead): $2.2k	Customer Lifetime Value(CLV): $1.2M
Average CPM (Cost-per-Impression): $4.14	Event / Webinar Attendees: 125	Marketing Sourced: Sales Pipeline Revenue: $2.9M	Marketing Sourced: Closed Won Revenue: $.4M
Share of Voice (media & social media) 20% & 12	Email Click Through Rates: 3.1%	Marketing Influenced: Sales Pipeline Revenue: $7.2M	Marketing Influenced: Closed Won Revenue: $1M
Pages Per Session: 2.3	Content Downloads: 650		Net Promoter Score: 68
SEO Authority Score: 79	CPC (Cost-per-Click): $.29		
	Total Conversions: 169		
DETERMINE KPI'S			
DETERMINE BENCHMARKS			

At the beginning of each quarter, assign a benchmark to each KPI and metric listed within your dashboard. Then, three months later as the quarter concludes, collect and gather all of the actual performance data for each of your KPI's and metrics (i.e. ad impressions, click-through-rates, MQL's generated) and see how your strategy is measuring up and performing against the benchmarks.

Before developing your KPI's and metrics, spend time really thinking through which KPI's and metrics you need to measure for your strategy. For instance, when it comes to assessing specific webpage performance it may be easy to want to track and measure any and all web pages, but that may not be realistic with your busy schedule; instead limit your tracking to only those pages that contain high-value content and/or to those pages where you are driving traffic.

When updated regularly, the Quarterly Performance Dashboard can be shared with other internal stakeholders as appropriate.

4. Chapter Bonus Material

Here are some additional best practices and bonus material specific to this chapter:

A/B Test

Not every ad you run, email you send, or content asset you publish will perform as you had hoped—that's why it's absolutely necessary to continuously *A/B test* the tactical components of your strategy. A/B testing is the testing of one variable to see which one performs better. For example, when deploying a mass email, consider splitting the email target list into two groups, and then create a different subject line or different message for each group to see which email generates the most opens, clicks, and overall engagements.

You can do this with ads, too. Run different ads that promote the same call-to-action but perhaps use different creative or copy and see which performs better. Try running them in different media channels and social media channels to see which one performs better. Overall, the goal here is to find the message, copy, or content and the channels that perform the best and focus your resources there. A/B testing is virtually unlimited in use and scope, but should always be a best practice for any B2B marketer.

Multivariate Testing

Multivariate testing should be done as well, where appropriate. Rather than A/B testing, which evaluates one variable, *multivariate testing* evaluates multiple variables. Multivariate is best for testing web content.

Here you can test different combinations of copy content, color, CTA location, navigation features, location, and more, to see which performs the best. You can measure success by evaluating the number of people who completed a call-to-action, time on page, or pages-per-session.

Think Pareto Principle

Apply the Pareto Principle (80 / 20 Rule) to your work. The *Pareto Principle* is the belief that 80% of the effects come from 20% of the causes. In a B2B marketing sense this would mean that 80% of your marketing results come from 20% of your marketing activities. As you execute on your strategy take a step back from time to time, reflect on your strategy, and make sure you are working on those activities and strategies that yield the best outcomes. Look for opportunities to refine your strategy; double your efforts on those that produce the best results, and eliminate or reduce those that do not. Then wait, step back, and look at it again.

Insider Tips

To help you better measure marketing performance here are a few resources I have personally found useful for me as a marketer, and that you may find useful too. As was mentioned in Chapter 3, **SiriusDecisions**, a consulting firm specializing in B2B marketing, sales, and product management, will likely be one of the best resources to help you find, determine, or create benchmarks if none are available. Rather than just being able to provide B2B industry average figures, they will likely be able to offer more data that's specific to your market, giving you a more targeted data set in which to work.

Tap into Google Tools to Monitor & Measure Performance

Google offers many tools to help you track the performance of your strategy. Google tools that help you manage online advertisements include **Google Adwords** and **Google Adwords Keyword Planner**. These tools will help you to build, manage, assess, and make adjustment to your paid media strategy on search engines. There is also **Google Analytics**, which will help you to better understand, monitor, and view all the web traffic visiting your site, including where the traffic originated, how long people stayed, what they did when they got to your site, where they exited, and much, much more.

Wrap Up

——————

Congratulations! You have finished the book, and if you completed each chapter's *Call-to-Action* using your working document, then you have also just created your very own marketing strategy. This will serve as the official working blueprint for your approach to the market. Even if you didn't complete the *Call-to-Action* exercises, my hope is that you still learned some valuable B2B marketing tips and best practices that will serve you well.

As an added bonus, if you wish to receive the completed *Marketing Strategy Working Document* template that was referenced throughout the book, contact me at jasonwsimmons.com and I will email it directly to you.

Thank you again for taking this journey with me and for reading this book. Good luck!

Lexicon

A/B Testing: The process of testing or comparing two versions of a web page, email subject line or similar in order to determine which performs the best.

Account-Based Marketing: A specific type of approach to B2B marketing, typically dealing with enterprise-wide sales deals that target each individual account as if it were its own market.

Anchor Content: This is a marketing asset piece that is rich in content and that can be spun into several smaller content assets for the purposes of maximizing exposure of a message, thereby anchoring a content strategy. White papers, research surveys, or eBooks are great examples of anchor content that can be turned to several smaller content assets such as several blog posts, webinars, social media posts, and more.

Authority (SEO Authority): A numerical value that predicts how well a specific web page may rank on search engine results pages (SERP's).

Average Cost-per-lead (CPL): The cost paid on average to produce one marketing qualified lead. It is calculated by taking the marketing budget devoted to all lead-gen initiatives or campaigns and dividing it by the total number of leads actually generated.

Average Customer Acquisition Cost: The total marketing cost paid on average to produce one paying client or won deal.

Awareness Phase: The first / early stage within the buyer's journey, and typically the stage when prospective buyers are still educating themselves on their work challenges or problems; also known as *Education Phase*.

Back-link: An incoming hyperlink that leads from one website or webpage to another website or webpage.

BANT: A common acronym used to define a qualified lead within the B2B Marketing Space. This refers to lead filters: Budget, Authority, Need, and Timeframe. Leads that meet approved BANT criteria are usually deemed ready for sales.

Benchmark: A benchmark is a reference, value, or metric against which KPI's can be compared or measured.

Bounce Rate: The percentage of visitors to a page or site who then leave or navigate away from the site. It is a single page session on a site.

Brand Guidelines: A set of guidelines that describes and defines the company brand and how the brand should be represented in the market via print, digital, and broadcast media.

Buyer Buzzwords: These are specific words and nomenclature that are related to the buyer's industry or buyer's job title.

Buyer Journey: The buyer journey is the path one travels when making a purchasing decision. Different types of content are needed to accommodate the buyer through each buying phase of the journey, and to help them seamlessly transition from one phase to the next. The three phases of the buyer's journey include *Awareness Phase, Consideration Phase,* and *Decision Phase.*

Call-to-Action: A common marketing request intended for prospective buyers or audiences to do something or engage in a desired action;

common CTA's include *read now, click here, watch video, learn more, download*, and similar.

Campaign Theme: The campaign theme is a specific message to the market that tells a story both about how a solution helps buyers, and why it is of value to the market. It can tell this story in a creative, fun, innovative, or imaginative way.

Click-Through-Rates (CTR's): The total number of clicks an ad receives divided by the total number of times that particular ad is shown (impression). A total of 20 clicks for an ad that had 1,000 impressions would equal 2% CTR.

Closed-Lost: An opportunity in the sales pipeline that did not result in a sale and was thus closed out.

Closed-Won: An opportunity in the sales pipeline that resulted in a sale and was then closed out.

Competitive Analysis: A competitive analysis is the evaluation of competitors' strengths and weaknesses relative to another competitor.

Consideration Phase: The second / middle-level stage within the buyer's journey when prospective buyers are typically evaluating competing brands and solutions.

Contact Us Form Submissions: The total number of people who complete a *contact us* form submission requesting to speak with a company representative. Also referred to as a "hand-raiser."

Content Atomization: The act of taking an anchor content piece and atomizing it into several smaller individual assets such as blogs, webinars, social media posts, and similar.

Content Downloads: The total number of people who download marketing content; typically gated content.

Conversion Rates: The number of conversions divided by the total number of ad clicks (actions taken). For instance, if an ad had 1,000 clicks and 35 conversions came from those clicks the conversion rate would be 3.5%.

Conversions: When someone clicks into an ad and then completes the call-to-action, such as download gated content or click into another page.

Cost-per-Action (CPA): The total cost spent on an ad divided by the total number of desired actions that came from that ad (for clarification, desired action would be the action that person took after clicking into that ad, -such as downloading gated content. This is the difference between cost-per-click and cost-per-action). For instance, an ad that costs $1,000 and received 16 desired actions would mean the cost-per-action is $62.50.

Cost-per-Click (CPC): The total cost or price paid for an advertisement divided by the number of clicks that ad receives. For example, an ad that costs $1,000 and received 320 clicks would equal $3.12 CPC.

Customer Lifetime Value: The calculated prediction of revenue gained from the future relationship with a client. Formula: Average annual revenue contributed by client, multiplied by average number of years a client remains a client, subtracted by the average customer acquisition cost.

Customer Relationship Management System: A software or web-based tool used to help organizations mange and process information/data for prospects and customers - such as prospect/customer data, interactions, and engagements. The purpose of which is to provide efficiencies in the sales process,

Decision Phase: The third / last-level stage within the buyer's journey, also known as the *purchase phase,* when prospective buyers are getting an up-close look at a product or solution, typically through demos, trials, or consultations.

Earned Media: Media activity generated by others through publicity or promotion; such as customers, third-party sources, or news outlets.

Editorial Calendar: A calendar used to help marketers plan, organize, and publish content, from ideation through creation through publication.

Email Click-Through Rates: The total number of unique clicks inside an email divided by the total number of email addresses that received that email. A total of 40 clicks in an email that had 1,000 email recipients would equal 4% email CTR.

Email Open Rates: The percentage of people on an email list (within an email campaign), who open a particular email.

End-Users: A buyer's customer or constituent and who is the ultimate user of a product, solution, or service.

Event & Webinar Attendees: The total number of attendees who attend an event, webinar, or some other face-to-face or direct virtual engagement.

Goal: A desired outcome one sets out to achieve.

Impression: A single display of an ad on a webpage.

Inbound Marketing (pull marketing): This refers to marketing activity that "pulls" prospects into a content or message. For instance, a paid search ad is clicked on by a prospective buyer who later turns into a marketing qualified lead for sales.

Influencers: Someone who has the ability to affect the decision-making process of a buyer (in most cases it is a buyer's professional colleague).

KPI (Key Performance Indicator): A key performance indicator is a quantifiable measurement of a particular activity that helps determine success in achieving a particular objective.

Marketing Automation System: A software or web-based tool that marketing departments use for the purpose of automating marketing actions. Such marketing actions include tasks such as email deployments, targeted display advertising, lead scoring, and monitoring individual web traffic though cookies.

Marketing-Influenced Closed-Won Revenue: Marketing-influenced pipeline revenue that later turned into closed-won deals.

Marketing-Influenced Pipeline Revenue / Marketing-Influenced Sales Opportunities: Revenue in the pipeline that was influenced by marketing activity but only after the initial lead had already been generated by sales (i.e. lead was acquired by sales through cold-call but later engaged in some sort of marketing activity such as attended a webinar, or downloaded marketing content).

Marketing Qualified Lead (MQL): A lead generated by marketing and that meets specific criteria as agreed upon between sales and marketing.

Marketing-Sourced Closed-Won Revenue: Marketing-sourced pipeline revenue that later turned into closed-won deals.

Marketing-Sourced Pipeline Revenue / Marketing-Sourced Sales Opportunities: Revenue in the pipeline that came from leads that were produced directly from marketing activity (i.e. lead came from content campaign and was nurtured and passed to sales).

Media Mix: The combination of all media types: paid media, owned media, earned media, and social media.

Media Share-of-Voice: The percentage of all web content mentions a particular brand or company receives relative to its competitors. If a particular brand was mentioned 100 times in the media and the total number of mentions among all brands was 500, the media share-of-voice would be 20%. 100/500 = 20%

Mobile-Usability / Mobile-Optimization (SEO Mobile-Usability): Websites that are adapted for mobile devices; websites which are not mobile-friendly result in poorer search rankings.

Multivariate Testing: Unlike A/B testing which tests one variable, multivariate testing considers multiple variables.

Net Promoter Score: A tool and measurement that is used to gauge customer loyalty by assessing how likely a client is to recommend a company or solution to others. NPS score is on a range of 1-100.

Nurture Campaign: Also referred to as drip campaign, a nurture campaign is a sequence of marketing emails delivered to prospective buyers for the purpose of engaging them with a branded message. Those who are actively consuming content in a nurture campaign may be ready to pass on to sales as a marketing qualified lead. Typically nurture or drip campaigns are triggered when someone fills out a form (and their email address was captured) to download a marketing content asset.

Objective: The desired-action needed to achieve a desired outcome.

Outbound Marketing (push marketing): This refers to marketing activity that "pushes" content and messages to prospects. For example, deploying an outbound marketing email, it is then opened by a prospective buyer who engages in the call-to-action, and later turns into a marketing qualified lead for sales.

Owned Media: Media activity gained through assets a company or organization owns and controls such as a company website, marketing content, or similar.

Pages-per-Session (average): The average number of pages viewed on a website site, within one site visit/session.

Paid Media: Media activity which is purchased; such as paid advertising, sponsorships, and similar.

Paid Search: Advertising that takes place on search engines.

Pareto Principle: The belief that 80% of the effects come from 20% of the causes.

Positioning Statement: A short but simple statement that best describes an organization's solution to the market while differentiating it from competitors and highlighting its value.

Professional Trade Association: An organization that operates in a specific industry and is usually founded or funded by businesses within that industry.

Relevancy (SEO Relevancy): The degree to which content on websites coincides with the keywords or search terms used. The more relevant web content is to the search terms used, the greater the chance of receiving a more favorable position on SERP's.

Remarketing Ads: These are targeted ads directed to those who have previously visited a website; as they continue browsing the Internet they will be served specific displays ads to bring them back to that website.

Return on Investment (ROI): Expressed as a percentage or ratio, it is the benefit of a particular investment divided by the cost of said investment.

Sales Accepted Lead (SAL): A marketing qualified lead that has been passed to the sales team and is awaiting approval and further qualification.

Sales Funnel Conversion: The rate at which leads convert in the sales funnel from one stage to the next: MQL to SAL to SQL to Closed Opportunity.

Sales Qualified Lead (SQL). A prospective client who has engaged with and been vetted by sales and has moved into a sales opportunity; it is the lead stage that follows Sales Accepted Lead.

Search Engine Marketing (SEM): A marketing strategy focused primarily on driving paid traffic to a particular website or landing page and is achieved through paid-media (i.e. paid search advertising, remarketing, and similar).

Search Engine Optimization (SEO): A marketing strategy focused primarily on driving organic traffic to a particular website or landing page and is achieved through improving organic positioning and ranking on SERP's (Search Engine Results Pages). Improving a website's organic position or ranking on SERP's is done by improving page authority, relevancy, and mobile-usability.

Shareable Content: Features on websites, landing pages, and other digital assets that allow for quick sharing of that content via social media channels, email, SMS text and other outlets.

Social Media 4-1-1 Rule: The rule that states for any given 6 social media posts, 4 should be re-sharing what others have posted (e.g. re-tweets, shares, or reposts); 1 should be a response or reply to a post of a follower; and 1 should be a post of one's own content that is pushed out into the market.

Social Media: Media activity gained on social media platforms

Social Media Shares & Engagements: The total number of engagements or actions taken on a social media post, such as liking, sharing, or retweeting.

Story-telling: Developing a marketing message that puts the end-user's story at the forefront of that message.

Tagline: A statement or phrase that represents a brand more so than the solution being sold by the brand; it projects what the brand does (even if not directly) while leaving a lasting impression.

Time on Page: The amount of time a visitor spends visiting a particular page on a website before leaving.

Tone-of-Voice: How a message is intended to come across and how it is to be interpreted by consumers of that message; it conveys feeling.

Top-of-Funnel Leads: The awareness phase of the buyer's journey. It is when prospective buyers begin to educate themselves on their challenges and issues, and seek specific content such as blogs, white papers, and research surveys, among others. Top-of-funnel leads will then progress to middle-of-funnel, which is the consideration phase of the buyer's journey, and then to bottom-of-funnel, which is the decision phase of the buyer journey.

Total Clicks (ads): The total number of clicks an ad receives.

Total Number of MQL's Generated: The total number of marketing qualified leads generated. It is the aggregate of all leads generated from all lead sources that stem from all lead-gen initiatives.

Total Page Views: The total number of views a particular webpage has received.

Value Proposition: A value proposition is a promise of value to be delivered. It's the primary reason a prospect should buy from you, and a clear statement that explains how your product solves customers' problems or improves their situation (relevancy); delivers specific benefits (quantified value); tells the ideal customer why they should buy from you and not from the competition (unique differentiation). (Laja, No Published Date Provided)

REFERENCES

Works Cited

Hanington, J. (2015, Februrary). *How to Create Brand Messaging that Really Resonates*. Retrieved April 1, 2017, from pardot.com: https://www.pardot.com/blog/how-to-create-brand-messaging-that-really-resonates/

Laja, P. (No Published Date Provided,). *ConversionXL blog page*. Retrieved December 22nd, 2016, from ConversionXL website: https://conversionxl.com/value-proposition-examples-how-to-create/

Whitler, K. A. (2015, February 5). *Are Today's Marketers Tomorrow's CEO's?* Retrieved July 15, 2016, from Forbes.com: https://www.forbes.com/sites/kimberlywhitler/2015/02/05/why-todays-marketers-are-tomorrows-ceos/#35179dfb3126

ABOUT THE AUTHOR

Jason is a passionate, experienced, and driven B2B marketing leader who has a track record of helping organizations achieve success. By creating and executing strategic marketing campaigns that align to organizational goals, that are built upon deep insights about the buyer, and that incorporate a balanced mix of paid, owned, earned, and social media – he is able to generate & influence pipeline revenue, improve brand favorability, and strengthen customer lifetime value.

He holds a Masters degree in Business Administration from the W. P. Carey School of Business at Arizona State University. He has also received various certifications through B2B Marketing firms such as SiriusDecisions and the Content Marketing Institute.

Jason lives in Phoenix, AZ with his wife Seela; they enjoy hiking, yoga, and traveling. They are both active in charities that help support, acclimate, and assist refugees who have newly arrived to the U.S.

Get in touch with Jason by visiting his website at jasonwsimmons.com